EXPLORE
THE ICE AGE!

Cindy Blobaum

Illustrated by Bryan Stone

More titles in the **Explore Your World!** Series

Check out more titles at www.nomadpress.net

Nomad Press
A division of Nomad Communications
10 9 8 7 6 5 4 3 2 1

Copyright © 2017 by Nomad Press. All rights reserved.
No part of this book may be reproduced in any form without permission in writing from
the publisher, except by a reviewer who may quote brief passages in a review or **for limited educational use**.
The trademark "Nomad Press" and the Nomad Press logo are trademarks of Nomad Communications, Inc.

This book was manufactured by Versa Press,
East Peoria, Illinois
October 2017, Job #J17-07605

ISBN Softcover: 978-1-61930-581-6
ISBN Hardcover: 978-1-61930-577-9

Educational Consultant, Marla Conn

Questions regarding the ordering of this book should be addressed to
Nomad Press
2456 Christian St.
White River Junction, VT 05001
www.nomadpress.net

Printed in the United States of America.

CONTENTS

Interested in primary sources? Look for this icon.

Use a smartphone or tablet app to scan the QR code and explore more!
You can find a list of URLs on the Resources page.

If the QR code doesn't work, try searching the Internet with
the Keyword Prompts to find other helpful sources.

KEYWORD PROMPTS

ice age

TIMELINE

C. 20,000 BCE: Glacial ice reaches its maximum size in the most recent ice age.

C. 9600 BCE: The most recent ice age ends.

C. 50 BCE: Roman poet Titus Lucretius Carus writes about the human use of stones and sticks as tools.

1300–1850: The world experiences what is often called the Little Ice Age, which isn't a true ice age but consists of periods of cold temperature broken up by warmer times.

1739 CE: French-Canadian soldier Charles LeMoyne becomes the first known European to see hundreds of Ice Age fossil bones in what is now known as Big Bone Lick in Kentucky.

1771: Johann Esper finds bear and lion bones and human bones in a cave in the Jura Mountains in southwestern Germany.

1788: One of the first fossil specimen of the giant ground sloth is found in Argentina.

1796: Georges Cuvier, a French scientist, gives one speech about mammoths being extinct relatives of elephants and another speech about giant sloths being extinct relatives of smaller sloths. He becomes known as the "Father of Paleontology."

1833: Two pieces of etched antlers are found in France.

JULY 1977: A Siberian miner uncovers Dima, a frozen baby mammoth, while bulldozing a patch of freshly thawed ground.

MAY 2007: Lyuba, an entire mummified baby mammoth, is found along the northern coast in Russia by a Nenets reindeer herder and his sons.

2009: A herd of pigs foraging for food in Scotland unearths a set of 12,000-year-old Ice Age stone tools.

1901: The owners of the La Brea Tar Pits in California let paleontologists remove bones from the area.

2015: A perfectly preserved mummified puppy is found in Siberian permafrost. The puppy is thought to have died in a landslide near a river.

1879: Cave paintings are discovered in the Altamira cave in northern Spain.

2016: Spanish scientists publish the first evidence that early humans hunted cave lions and used their pelts to cover huts used for important rituals.

1837: Swiss scientist Louis Agassiz presents his theory of a great ice age to a group of geologists. He becomes known as the "Father of the Ice Age."

JULY 2017: The perfectly preserved bodies of a Swiss couple who went missing 75 years earlier are found on a shrinking glacier in Switzerland.

INTRODUCTION

WELCOME TO THE ICE AGE!

Imagine being alive around 12,000 years ago. Icy glaciers that were more than a mile tall inched their way across much of the earth. Giant hairy mammoths roamed the land. Fierce saber-toothed cats and short-faced bears prowled in search of food.

Stone Age people worked together to find food, make shelters, invent tools, paint caves, and explore new places. Welcome to the end of the Ice Age, when the world was colder, many animals were bigger, and life was harder than it is today.

WORDS TO KNOW

glacier: a large body of ice moving slowly down a slope or valley or spreading outward on a land surface.

shelter: a place to live that protects a person from the weather.

Ice Age: a period of time when glaciers covered a large part of the earth.

1

Even though humans were alive during the Ice Age, they couldn't take photos, write books, or make videos of their lives. They didn't have the right tools! As the earth warmed up and life changed, people forgot the way things used to be.

People made up stories to explain the strange things they found around them. People who lived in Greece found giant mammoth skulls with holes in the middle. Since they had never seen a mammoth, they said the skulls were from one-eyed monsters called cyclops.

People in Germany found skulls with big teeth and thought they were from dragons. In Denmark, old stories said huge, strange rocks found in the middle of fields were thrown there by giants. Other groups have said the huge rocks were dropped in fields by aliens or floods.

· DID YOU KNOW? · · · · · · · · · · · ·

Find something you don't recognize around your house or school. Make up a story to explain what you think it is before you ask someone else to identify it. How close is your guess?

Since the 1800s, scientists have been doing studies to learn more about the Ice Age and to explain the objects people have found. Scientists study the following things.

* rock layers around the world

* bones and frozen bodies that have been found

* ancient art found in caves

* Earth's orbit around the sun

Many scientists believe that the world has been cycling in and out of ice ages for about 2.6 million years. There would be many cold years, followed by periods of warmer years. They believe this cycle of warming and cooling may have happened more than 100 times, with some cycles being longer and colder than others." This book focuses on the most recent ice age, which ended about 10,000 years ago.

orbit: the path that Earth takes around the sun.

cycle: a repeated series of events.

WORDS TO KNOW

A HUMAN-MADE GLACIER!

During the winter of 2014–2015, more than 110 inches of snow fell in the Boston, Massachusetts, area. The city scooped up a lot of the snow and made a huge pile 75 feet high. This was like a human-made glacier. The pile of snow didn't completely melt until July 14, 2015!

PS **You can see a news program about this pile of snow.**

KEYWORD PROMPTS

Boston snow melts

equator: an imaginary line around the middle of the earth.

theory: an unproven idea that explains why something is the way it is.

WORDS ⊚ KNOW

THE TILT OF THE EARTH

What causes the cold years? Our sun is a source of heat for the whole world. Unless you live near the equator, the amount of sun that reaches your home changes during different seasons.

During the summer, you get more sun because your part of the earth is tilted toward the sun. In the winter, you get less sun because your part of the earth is tilted away from the sun. This is why it's warmer in the summer and colder in the winter!

Through careful observations and measurements, scientists developed the theory that the amount to which the earth tilts changes. During an ice age, the earth doesn't tilt as much as it does at other times. This means the areas near the North and South Poles don't get as much sun during their summers.

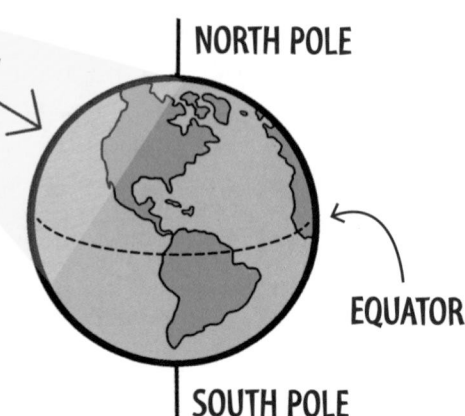

NORTH POLE

EQUATOR

SOUTH POLE

DECEMBER

JUNE

NORTH POLE

EQUATOR

SOUTH POLE

During some of these times, the orbit of Earth also changed. Instead of going in a circle around the sun, Earth followed a path like a giant oval. That means during some years, Earth was closer to the sun than during other years.

When we are farther away from the sun during the winter, it gets colder. When we are farther away from the sun in the summer, it doesn't warm up as much. What if it snows a lot during the winter and the land doesn't get as much sun during the summer? The snow will pile up so much it creates glaciers.

How the Ice Age started is just the beginning. In *Explore the Ice Age!*, you'll learn about where all that ice came from and where it went when the Ice Age ended.

WHY DID THE WOOLLY MAMMOTH CROSS THE ROAD?

HA HA HA!

To get to the other glacier!

Have you ever seen the *Ice Age* movies? Was that what life was really like during the Ice Age? How did people, animals, and plants living near the glaciers survive? To investigate these questions and more, grab some gear and let's get started!

INVESTIGATE THE ICE AGE!

Each chapter of this book begins with a question to help guide your exploration of the Ice Age. Keep the question in your mind as you read the chapter. Record your thoughts, questions, and observations in a science journal. At the end of each chapter, use your science journal to think of answers to the questions. Does your answer change as you read the chapter?

? **INVESTIGATE!**

Why is it cold in the winter and warm in the summer in many places?

reflector: a material that reflects light.

reflect: to bounce back.

WORDS ⓣⓞ **KNOW**

GOOD SCIENCE PRACTICES

Every good scientist keeps a science journal. Do the project on page 7 to make a special Ice Age science journal. As you read through this book, you will do many other projects. For each project, make and use a scientific method worksheet, like the one shown here. Scientists use the scientific method to keep their experiments organized. A scientific method worksheet will help you keep track of your observations and results.

Step	Example
1. Question: What am I trying to find out? What problem am I trying to solve?	How much does a **reflector** slow the melting of ice?
2. Research: What information is already known?	A science study says ice **reflects** up to 85 percent of sunlight.
3. Hypothesis/Prediction: What do I think the answer will be?	I think the ice under the reflector will take twice as long to melt.
4. Equipment: What supplies do I need?	journal, pencil, 2 ice cubes, trays, reflector, timer
5. Method: What steps will I follow?	Put each ice cube on a tray in the sun. Cover one with reflector. Time how long it takes for each one to melt.
6. Results: What happened and why?	The one under the reflector took a lot longer to melt. I wonder if the results are the same when the temperature is warmer or cooler.

ICE AGE JOURNAL

Just like the glaciers worked as reflectors, your journal will reflect what you learn as you do the activities in this book! The basic design is special—you will use the covers to do some of the projects!

SUPPLIES

* 2 flat pieces of foam the same size (meat trays work fine)
* scissors
* pencil
* paper
* hole punch
* aluminum foil
* glue
* 2–3 twist ties

1 Make sure the pieces of foam are clean and dry. Use the scissors to cut off any edges that turn up. You want the pieces to be as flat as possible. These will become the covers of your notebook.

2 Use the pencil to make two holes along one edge of one piece of foam. Be sure to make the holes about ½ inch from the edge so they don't tear through the edge.

3 Put the piece of foam with the holes on top of the piece of foam without holes. Push the pencil through each hole to mark where the holes on piece two should be, then use the pencil to make the holes.

4 To make filler paper for your notebook, put blank paper under one piece of foam and trace around it. Cut around the inside edge of the line you drew. Do this with at least 10 pieces of paper.

5 Use the holes on a foam tray as a guide for where to punch holes on your sheets of paper.

THIS PROJECT CONTINUES ON THE NEXT PAGE ⟶

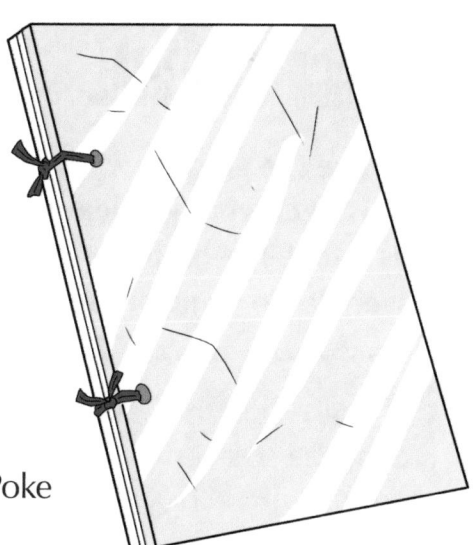

6 Tear off a piece of aluminum foil that is big enough to wrap around both sides of one foam piece. Put the aluminum foil shiny side down on a table. Cover one side of the foam piece with a thin layer of glue. Put the foam about 1 inch from the edge of the foil. Use a pencil to poke the holes through the foil. Cover the top side of the foam with glue. Wrap the aluminum foil around the foam. Poke holes where needed.

7 Line up the holes as you make your notebook with the paper and covers (one cover has aluminum foil and the other does not). Poke a twist tie through each hole. Twist the ends around each other to hold it all together. Use your journal for the activities in this book!

BIG ICE, BIG WORDS

Scientists use two big words when they talk about the Ice Age. They call it the **Pleistocene** period when they are talking about the **geology** of the earth. When they are talking about early people, they use the word **Paleolithic** to describe people from this time.

WORDS TO KNOW

Pleistocene: the time in the earth's history from about 2.5 million years ago to 10,000 years ago that experienced repeated ice ages.

geology: the study of the earth and its rocks. A geologist studies geology.

Paleolithic: describes humans and their ancestors who used stone tools, until about 10,000 years ago. Also called the Stone Age.

PROJECT!

REFLECTION

SUPPLIES

* 2 plastic lids
* 2 same-sized ice cubes
* a sunny day or two lamps
* Ice Age journal
* pencil

If you have been around a lot of clean ice and snow during the day, you know it can be hard to see because it is so bright. Ice acts as a reflector. When the sun's rays hit clean ice, most of them bounce back up into space. This makes it harder for the sun to warm things up.

1 Place an ice cube on top of each plastic lid and place each lid in a sunny spot or under a lamp. If you are using lamps, make sure each lid is the same distance away from the light bulb.

2 Remove one sheet of paper from your Ice Age journal. Open your journal so the foil side is over one lid and the plain side is over the other.

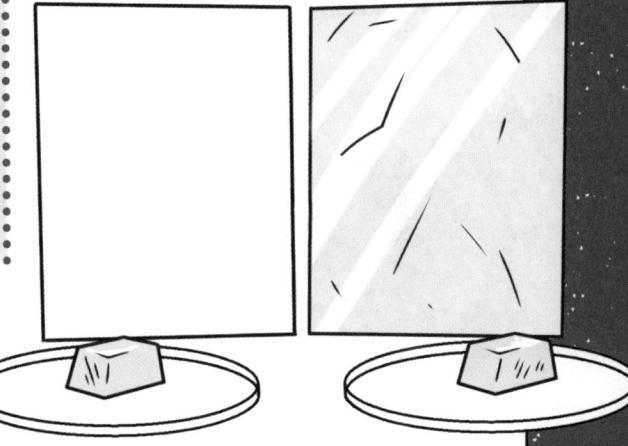

3 Start a scientific method worksheet. Record the time you are starting the experiment and your predictions. Which ice cube will melt faster? How much faster will it melt? Check on your ice cubes every few minutes. Record your observations and the times you make them.

TRY THIS! Scientists know that when ice gets covered by wind-blown dirt, it absorbs the sun's rays and warms up. Repeat the experiment, but sprinkle dark soil on the foil. Does that change your results?

CHAPTER 1

WHAT A WORLD!

When you say Ice Age, do you imagine the entire world covered in ice? What would that look like? How would anything grow? Where would you get food? How would you stay warm?

It is a good thing that the entire world wasn't covered in ice after all! During the Ice Age, about 30 percent of Earth's land was covered in ice.

? INVESTIGATE!

How much of the land where you live can't be used by plants and animals because it is covered by buildings or concrete?

ice pack: a large area of ice formed during a period of many years and made of pieces driven together by wind, weather, moving glaciers, water, and other forces.

WORDS TO KNOW

That means 70 percent of Earth was free of ice. Plants, animals, and people could live in many of these ice-free areas.

The amount of land that was covered in ice changed from season to season. During the winter, the ice pack could grow and cover more land. During the summer, some of the ice pack might melt and cover less land. But there was still was a lot of ice!

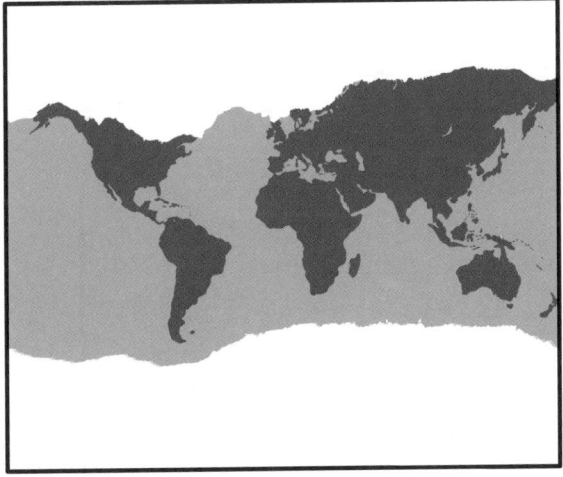

THE EARTH DURING THE ICE AGE

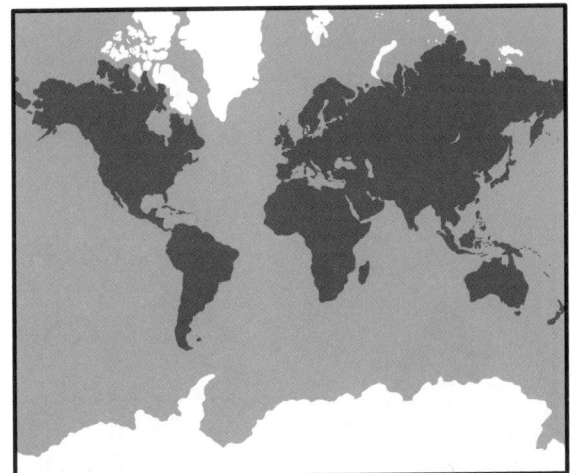

THE EARTH TODAY

MAKING ICE

Where did all that ice come from? During the Ice Age, snow, sleet, and hail fell during the winter. A lot of it fell in certain places, such as the Arctic, Antarctica, and on top of tall mountains. Since it did not warm up much in the summer, most of the snow and ice did not melt.

> **water cycle:** the continuous movement of water from the earth to the clouds and back to the earth again.
>
> **WORDS TO KNOW**

The next year, more snow, sleet, and hail fell. Again, it did not get warm enough in the summer to melt it all. This went on for thousands of years! As the different forms of frozen water piled higher, they got squished together and transformed into ice. In some places in Canada, the ice grew to be 2 miles high!

While the ice was piling up higher and higher, the water level in the oceans was getting lower and lower. Why do you think this happened? All that ice was made of water, and all that water was part of the **water cycle**.

DID YOU KNOW?

About 97 percent of the world's water is in the oceans.

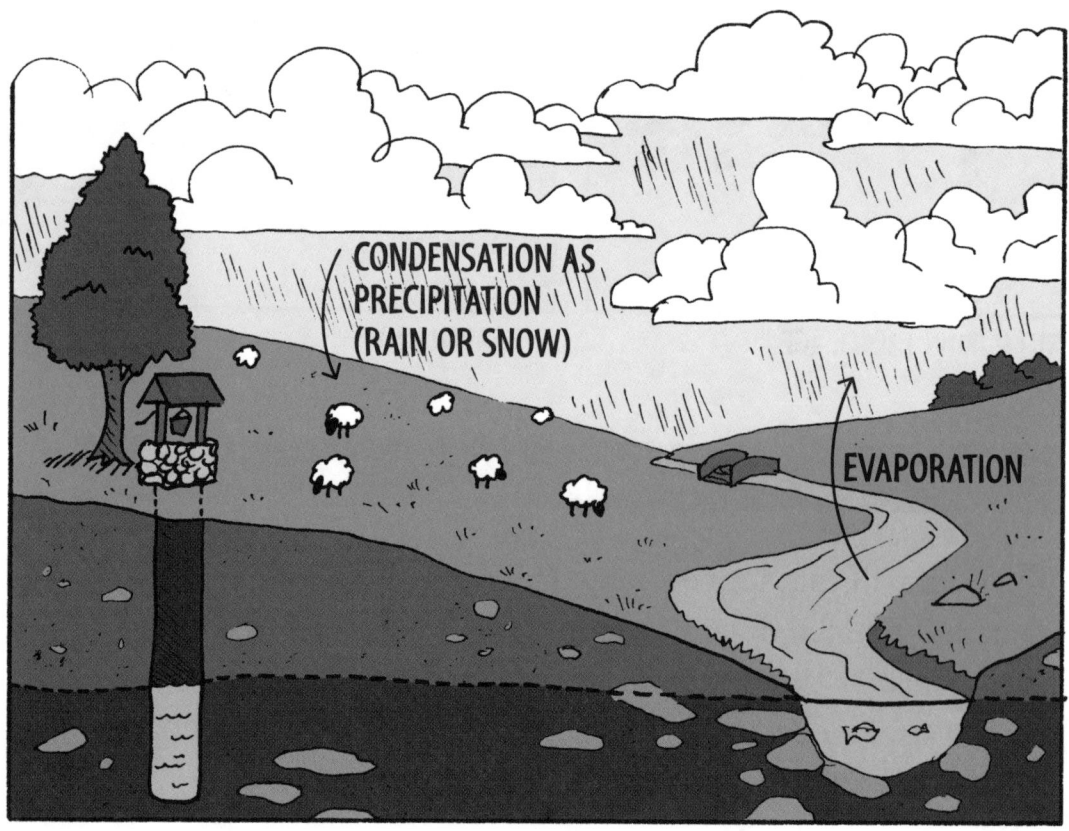

CONDENSATION AS PRECIPITATION (RAIN OR SNOW)

EVAPORATION

evaporate: when a liquid heats up and changes into a gas, or vapor.

water vapor: water as a gas, such as fog, steam, or mist.

condense: when a gas cools down and changes into a liquid.

WORDS ⊙ KNOW

Most of the water in the water cycle comes from the oceans! As more ice formed, there was less water for the oceans.

Water is always changing form and moving around the earth. When water is warm, it is a liquid. When water is very cold, it can freeze into a solid, called ice. Both warm and cold water can evaporate and become an invisible gas called water vapor. This is the water in the air.

WHERE CAN YOU FIND AN OCEAN WITHOUT ANY WATER?

HA HA HA!

On a map!

Warmer air can hold more water vapor than cooler air can hold. When wind moves warmer water vapor to a cooler area, the water vapor condenses and gets heavier. It falls out of the sky as precipitation: rain, snow, sleet, or hail.

That water runs into rivers, seeps into the ground, and gets drunk by thirsty animals. If it's snow or ice, it piles up on the ground or melts.

LOOK AROUND!

Look around to see if you can find where water has moved things in your area. Good things to look for include the following.

- Watch for signs of where waves came up on a beach.
- After a rain, see if you can tell where the water ran down the sidewalk, lawns, and street.
- If you live where it snows, watch the piles left by the snowplows.

estimate: a best guess using facts you know.

Beringia: the land between Siberia and Alaska that was exposed during the last ice age.

At the same time, water is always evaporating from solid ice or liquid water into the air as water vapor. This constant moving around of water is called the water cycle.

Have you ever been swimming in a swimming pool? It goes from shallow to deep pretty quickly. Unlike swimming pools, many ocean coasts have gentle slopes. Scientists estimate that when the ice was the thickest on the land, the water level in the oceans dropped by 400 feet. This means the coasts along New York and New Jersey were up to 70 miles farther away into what is now the ocean.

The same thing happened all over Earth. Britain is now an island, but during the Ice Age, it was connected to the rest of Europe. Today, parts of Alaska and Siberia have only 51 miles of seawater between them. When the sea level dropped during the Ice Age, the two countries were connected by a land bridge. That land bridge is known as Beringia.

IT'S A LAND BRIDGE. IT'S LIKE A BRIDGE... MADE OF LAND.

force: a push or pull applied to an object that changes an object's motion.

pressure: the force made when something pushes against something else.

WORDS ⊕ KNOW

ON THE MOVE

As the ice piled up, it got heavier. Push your hand down on a bare leg. Push hard! What do you feel? It doesn't take long before the force on your skin makes it feel a little warm. This warmth is created by the pressure.

Even though ice is cold, the pressure of a stack of ice 2 miles thick made the ice on the bottom just a bit warmer than the ice on top. What happens when ice warms up? It melts! That created a thin layer of water that the glacier could float on.

The glaciers that first started forming near the North and South Poles and at the tops of tall mountains didn't stay where they started. As the ice piled up, the glaciers pushed out farther and farther at the base. Often, the ice only moved about 3 feet a day, but sometimes it might go as far as 90 feet in one day!

RELEASE THE HOUNDS!

Today, as the earth warms up, glaciers are melting. Things that have been frozen inside glaciers for thousands of years are now becoming visible. Rocks, frozen animals, and even human-made tools have been released by melting glaciers.

You can see a cave lion that was released from ice here.

KEYWORD PROMPTS

cave lion National Geographic 🔍

tundra: the treeless Arctic land that is permanently frozen below the top layer of soil.

WORDS TO KNOW

This ice didn't stop for anything. It acted like a giant plow or bulldozer, pushing over everything in its path. Plants, trees, animals, even hills of soil and rocks were pushed flat by the moving ice. The glaciers pushed through mountains and made new valleys. Trees, rocks, and even animals got picked up and carried by the ice. Some of this stuff got stuck in the ice. The only way they could get out was if the ice melted.

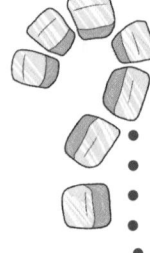

· DID YOU KNOW? · · · ·

Today, about 10 percent of Earth's land is covered in ice. That is equal to 5.8 million square miles.

TUNDRA

People, plants, and animals could not live and grow on the glaciers. It was hard living anywhere near the glaciers! The glaciers kept the air cold in summer and winter. Some scientists think it was also very windy and dry. Glaciers also kept the land near the glaciers almost frozen all year long. This land near glaciers is called the tundra.

MOVIE FACT CHECK

In the first *Ice Age* movie, Sid sees many things frozen in a block of ice—even a flying saucer. Glaciers can carry many things, but glacier ice is not clear! It looks more like snow cone ice than a clear ice cube.

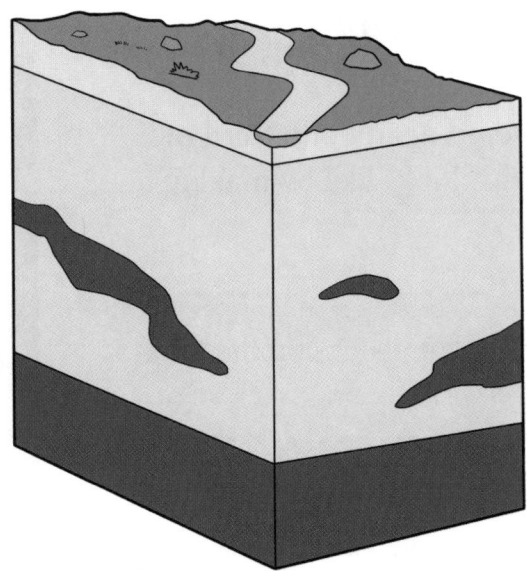

ACTIVE LAYER

PERMAFROST

permafrost: the tundra's permanently frozen layer of soil just beneath the surface of the ground.

WORDS TO KNOW

Tundra is different from other land. During the summer, the top part of the land warms enough to become soft. This is the active layer, where small plants, such as mosses, grasses, and low shrubs, can grow. About 6 feet down, the ground is still frozen solid. This land is called permafrost.

During the Ice Age and today, people living on the tundra get most of their food from hunting animals. Some of those animals need plants to eat. A single mammoth could eat between 130 and 660 pounds of food every day!

The earth during the Ice Age was a very different place from what we're used to today! But how do we know about a time period that was so long ago? We'll learn about that in the next chapter.

? CONSIDER AND DISCUSS

It's time to consider and discuss: How much of the land where you live can't be used by plants or animals because it is covered by buildings or concrete?

CHANGING WATER, CHANGING LAND

During the Ice Age, ice covered nearly one-third of the earth's land. See what this looks like by making a model.

SUPPLIES

* large clear plastic box or container
* Lego base sheets and blocks
* water
* ice cubes
* paper cup
* freezer
* Ice Age journal
* colored pencils

1 Put the biggest base sheet that fits, inside the box. This will be the ocean floor.

2 If you have more base sheets, stack them up on the bottom one to make your land. The more you have, the better.

3 Add colored blocks to make mountains, cliffs, and other land forms.

4 Pour enough water in the box to cover the lowest base sheet. Add more water so that it reaches halfway up your lowest block.

5 Add 4 to 6 ice cubes to one end of the box to show today's glaciers. Mark the water level on the blocks above water.

6 Sketch your land in your Ice Age journal.

7 Take out the Lego land and pour some of the water from the box into the paper cup. Put the cup into the freezer along with the ice cubes. Put the Lego land back into the box and water.

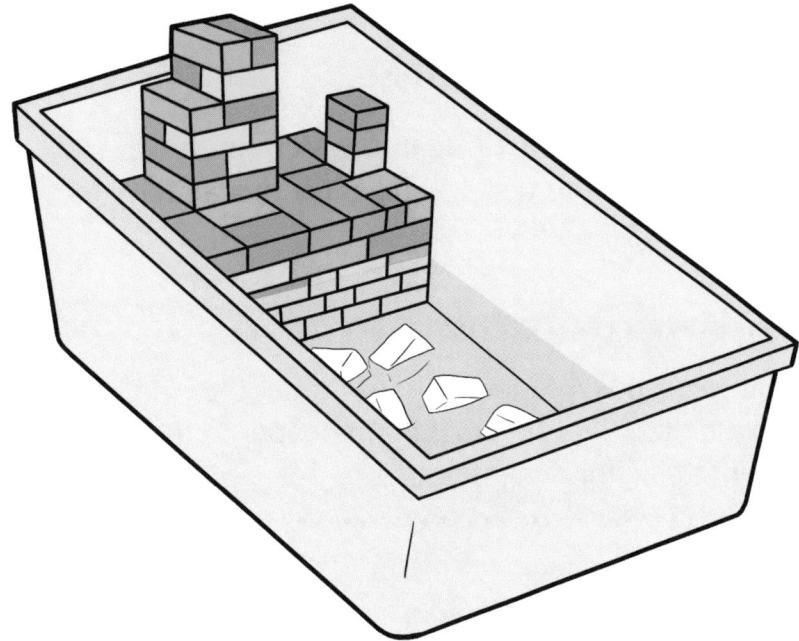

8 When the water in the cup has frozen, cut off the paper. You have made a model glacier.

9 Put this large glacier and the ice cubes on top of your land. This models an ice pack such as those found in the Ice Age. Check your marker lines to see how the water level has changed. Sketch what you see in your journal.

10 Watch the water level as the ice melts. Does it get back up to the marks you made on the blocks?

TRY THIS! Ice can be heavy! Put a layer of marshmallows under your Lego base sheet before you put the ice on top. Measure the height of the Lego base before and after you add the ice. What do you notice?

PROJECT!

WATER CYCLE WONDERS

We might think of ice melting into water, but how about ice turning into water vapor? Try this activity to see ice at work!

SUPPLIES

* shallow plastic tub
* paper
* scissors
* pencil
* ice cube
* freezer
* Ice Age journal

1 Cut the piece of paper so it fits in the bottom of the plastic tub. Put the tub with the paper in the freezer to chill for a few minutes.

2 Take the tub out of the freezer and the paper out of the tub. Put an ice cube on top of the paper. Trace around the ice cube as close and as quickly as you can. Put the paper with the ice cube on it back in the tub and in the freezer.

3 Start a scientific method worksheet in your Ice Age journal. What do you think will happen to the ice cube? Check the ice cube once a week.

4 What happens to the ice cube? What happens to the paper? Record your results in your journal.

WHAT'S HAPPENING? Do you find any **evidence** of water on your paper? Is the ice cube getting smaller? Where is the ice going? The ice is turning into a gas called water vapor in your freezer! This happens because the air in the freezer is usually very dry.

WORDS TO KNOW

evidence: something that supports the existence of something or the truth of an idea.

PROJECT!

GLACIERS ON THE GO!

Glaciers do not sit still! Instead, they are always on the move, even if they move very slowly. Try these experiments to see a much smaller version of glaciers on the go!

SUPPLIES

* sand or small pebbles
* plastic or cardboard drink carton
* water
* freezer
* scissors
* sloping outdoor area with soil, sand, or grass
* Ice Age journal

1 Put a handful of small pebbles or sand in the drink carton. Fill the carton about half full with water. Place the carton in a freezer for 3 to 4 hours. Overnight works best.

2 After the water has completely turned to ice, remove the carton from the freezer. Take it outside. Cut off the carton.

3 In your Ice Age journal, sketch the area where you are going to put the mini-glacier. Put the glacier on the ground. Push down hard and move it downhill as far as you want. When you stop, leave the glacier in place and let it melt.

4 Sketch the area again. What do you notice?

THINK ABOUT IT: When glaciers move, they flatten the land they cross. They also create ridges of rocks, soil, and plants in front of them and on each side. Geologists use these ridges to map the paths that glaciers took thousands of years ago.

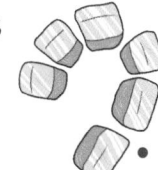

DID YOU KNOW?

Long Island, New York, is made of rocks and soil that were carried by glaciers in the most recent ice age!

COLD GARDEN

Today, gardeners can plant lettuce, peas, carrots, radishes, beets, broccoli, and other cool-season crops when the ground is still cold, but not frozen. This kind of ground is a bit like the tundra when it starts to thaw. To see how this works, try to start some seeds in your refrigerator!

SUPPLIES

* ✳ 2 clear cups
* ✳ paper towels
* ✳ scissors
* ✳ ruler
* ✳ permanent marker
* ✳ seeds for the cool season (lettuce, peas, radishes)
* ✳ seeds for the warm season (tomato, beans, corn)
* ✳ water
* ✳ plastic wrap
* ✳ 2 rubber bands
* ✳ refrigerator
* ✳ Ice Age journal
* ✳ pencil

1 Fold each paper towel so that it just fits around the inside of each clear cup. Cut off any extra.

2 Lay the paper towels flat. Use the ruler to measure up 2 inches from the bottom edge of each towel. Use the marker to draw a line.

3 Make separate piles of five seeds of each cool-season plant above the line on one paper towel. Use the marker to write the type of seed under the line under each pile.

4 Make separate piles of five seeds of each warm-season plant above the line on the other paper towel. Use the marker to write the type of seed under each pile.

5 Pour a small amount of water on each paper towel. This will help the seeds stay in place and start to grow.

PROJECT!

6 Place one paper towel in each cup with the seeds facing out. Cover each cup with a piece of plastic wrap. Use a rubber band to hold the plastic wrap in place. Put each cup in the refrigerator.

7 Start a scientific method worksheet in your Ice Age journal. Predict how long you think it will take for each type of seed to sprout. Record your predictions in your journal.

8 Check on your seeds every day. Record your observations in your journal. After plants have sprouted, take them out of the refrigerator. If you want to keep them growing, add soil to the cup. Put the cup in a sunny window. Keep in mind, not every seed will sprout!

TRY THIS! Repeat this experiment keeping the seeds in a sunny window instead of the refrigerator. Do you get different results?

THINK ABOUT IT: In the movie *Ice Age*, Manny and Sid get a watermelon for the young boy to eat. Do you think watermelons could grow near a glacier? Create an experiment with watermelon seeds in your refrigerator.

You can see an Ice Age garden at this website.

KEYWORD PROMPTS

Ice Age garden 🔍

MAKE A CLOUD

What's in the sky when it's raining or snowing? How does water vapor in the air turn into clouds and rain? Do this project to create your own cloud!

SUPPLIES

* ✳ 2-liter clear plastic bottle with cap
* ✳ warm water
* ✳ matches
* ✳ Ice Age journal
* ✳ pencil

Caution: Have an adult help you with the matches. Never use matches on your own.

1 Fill the bottle about one-third full with warm water. Put the cap on the bottle and squeeze it a few times. You are making water vapor go into the air.

2 As you take the cap off the bottle, have an adult light a match. Hold the match over the bottle and blow it out. Drop the smoking match into the bottle.

3 Quickly put the cap back on and squeeze the bottle a few times. What happens? Record your observations in your Ice Age journal.

THINK ABOUT IT: To make a cloud, water vapor needs something to stick to. The smoke from the match is tiny specks of dust and ash. When you squeeze the bottle, you mix the water vapor and dust. The water vapor sticks to the dust and makes a cloud you can see.

CHAPTER 2

DISCOVERING THE ICE AGE

How do we know there was an Ice Age? After all, there are no books, photographs, or emails from that long ago. There might not be a written record, but the glaciers, people, and animals from that time left behind clues.

We can study rocks from different places to figure out what happened when glaciers moved. Bodies and bones from animals have been found and studied.

? INVESTIGATE!

Why was it hard for people to believe the ice age theory at first?

artifact: an object made by people in the past, including tools, pottery, and jewelry.

fossil: the remains or traces of ancient life, including plants and animals.

culture: the beliefs and way of life of a group of people.

climate: the average weather patterns in an area during a long period of time.

WORDS ⊚ KNOW

People who lived at that time made tools, clothes, shelters, and art. Some buried their dead. Artifacts from these activities tell us where people and certain animals lived, what they ate, and how they changed through time.

Each clue is like a piece to a giant puzzle. Scientists look at the clues and try to make sense of them all.

SCIENTISTS TO KNOW!

Many different scientists study the world and have contributed to our understanding of the Ice Age. Did you ever think about being one of these scientists?

PALEONTOLOGISTS study the plants and animals that lived long ago. They do this by looking at fossils.

ARCHAEOLOGISTS study ancient people. They look at the artifacts left behind, such as tools, pottery, jewelry, and buildings.

ANTHROPOLOGISTS study all parts of past and present human behavior and cultures, including houses, food, clothing, language, art, and more.

GEOLOGISTS study the history of the earth and its life as revealed through rocks.

CLIMATE SCIENTISTS study climate patterns that happen during long periods of time.

GEOLOGISTS START THE STUDY

The first scientists to talk about the Ice Age were geologists in Europe. They wondered why big and small rocks were found far away from where they belonged. Some rocks that were usually found near the ocean were discovered high in the mountains. Rocks from mountains were found miles away in flat fields. Some of these rocks were as big as houses. How did these rocks get to places where they hadn't formed naturally? Geologists wanted to know!

Geologists also compared the ways rocks and land looked. Smaller rocks and pebbles covered the bottoms of streams and rivers or made giant piles in long lines. Huge flat rocks had deep lines grooved across their surfaces. Mountain chains in northern Europe had wide, U-shaped valleys. Mountain chains farther south had steep V-shaped valleys. Why?

DID YOU KNOW?

A scientist named Louis Agassiz (1808–1873) wrote a book and gave speeches about the Ice Age. He worked hard to convince most scientists to believe that, long ago, ice had covered Europe. For all his hard work, Agassiz is considered the "Father of the Ice Age."

iceberg: a large piece of floating ice.

WORDS TO KNOW

Geologists talked with people who lived near glaciers. They studied all different rocks. Some scientists suggested that ice had moved the rocks across most of Europe thousands of years earlier. For a long time, many people didn't believe that ice ages had happened. Eventually, scientists developed more tools to help support theories about ice ages, and now we know the ice ages occurred.

Geologists are still studying clues from the Ice Age. Smaller glaciers can be seen in high mountains all over the world, plus over Antarctica, Iceland, Greenland, and near the Arctic.

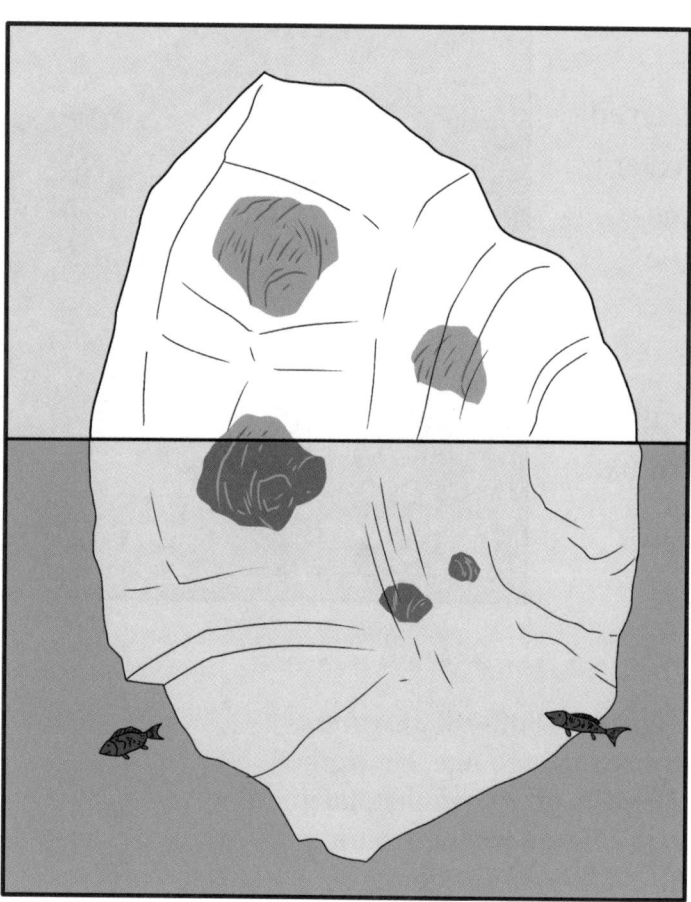

Every time a glacier melts, more rocks and sand wash out. Some glaciers get all the way to the sea, where they form a layer on the ocean floor. Geologists study the layers to see what is in them and how old they are. They also study rocks that were carried far out into the oceans by icebergs.

ANIMAL EVIDENCE

extinct: when a group of plants or animals dies out and there are no more left in the world.

WORDS TO KNOW

All around the world, people have been finding fossil evidence of strange animals. In 1796, scientist Georges Cuvier (1769–1832) studied a large bone that had been found along a river in Argentina. He compared it to bones from other animals, and said the bones were from a giant sloth.

Cuvier thought that type of sloth would never be found alive again. He was one of the first people to suggest that an animal might be extinct!

WHERE DO ROCKS GO FOR SUMMER VACATION?

HA HA HA!

Pebble Beach!

In the United States, Native Americans in the Kentucky area knew of a salty, swampy place where there were lots of huge bones on the ground. In 1807, President Thomas Jefferson asked explorer William Lewis to visit Kentucky and bring back mammoth bones and any other kinds of bones he could find. More people were beginning to believe the idea that giant animals had once walked the land.

MOVIE FACT CHECK

Sid the sloth, a main character in the *Ice Age* movies is much too small. The giant sloth bones paleontologists have found from the Ice Age would make Sid almost as tall as Manny the mammoth!

29

In the late 1800s, people in California collected tar from pits to seal their roofs. They found bones in the tar. At first, they thought the bones were from animals they saw every day. By 1901, a local geologist convinced others that many of the bones they were finding were from ancient animals.

In 1913, a family that owned one of these tar pits allowed scientists to dig for fossils. Since then, more than 600 types of Ice Age animal and plant fossils have been found in what is now called the La Brea Tar Pits.

People in Siberia and other northern places have found more than just bones. At times, animals died near a glacier. Instead of getting eaten by other animals or rotting into the soil, these animals were frozen in ice. When they emerge from the melting ice, scientists can study their bones, hair, skin, hearts, stomachs, brains, lungs—everything! Scientists have even found pieces of buttercup flowers between the teeth of a mammoth head found in Alaska.

DID YOU KNOW?

A rock that is moved far away from where it was made is called an erratic. One of the most famous glacial erratics in the United States is Plymouth Rock in Massachusetts. This is where the first Pilgrims are said to have set foot in America.

STONE AGE TOOLS AND ART

Not only have people found animal bones, they have found evidence from Ice Age humans. All around the world, people have discovered ancient spear points, spear throwers, arrowheads, hammerstones, scrapers, axes, needles, and beads. These were made from rocks, bones, antlers, and shells. Ice age people used these tools to hunt, make their homes and clothes, and to create art.

Stone tools offer lots of clues. If the rocks that the tools are made from are different from the rocks where they are found, we know the people traveled or traded. A mastodon bone with a spear point still stuck in it proves that

people hunted big animals. By looking at the size and design of the stone tool, archaeologists and anthropologists can estimate when it was made.

TREASURE REVEALED

Because the world's climate has been warming up, glaciers are melting fast. Every year, new frozen animals emerge from the ice and give us more clues about the last ice age. In Siberia alone, freeze-dried mummies of an Ice Age steppe bison, woolly rhinoceros, Przewalski's horse, puppy, and several mammoths have been found!

TOUR THE LASCAUX CAVES

In 1940, four boys were playing in the woods in France when their dog disappeared. They discovered the dog had slipped through a tiny hole in the ground into what is now known as the Lascaux Caves. These are caves where ancient people painted the walls with images of bison, stag, oxen, and other animals around 15,000 BCE.

You can take a virtual tour of the caves here.

KEYWORD PROMPTS

Lascaux Caves virtual tour

In 1833, a doctor found two ancient antlers in a cave near France's border with Switzerland. Then, in 1879, a cave full of paintings of extinct animals was found in Altamira, Spain.

At first, people didn't believe that humans from that long ago could make these pictures. But as scientists studied the paintings in Spain and ones found in other caves, people started thinking of the art as evidence of the Ice Age. Since then, Ice Age paintings and art have been found in more than 300 caves in Europe, as well as in a few caves in the Americas.

It's fascinating to see pictures of animals that lived thousands of years ago! In the next chapter, we'll learn more about the animals that not only survived during the Ice Age, but thrived.

 CONSIDER AND DISCUSS

It's time to consider and discuss: Why was it hard for people to believe the ice age theory at first?

PROJECT!

GLACIAL GUSH

SUPPLIES
* Ice Age journal
* pencil
* bucket
* sand
* small pebbles
* rocks
* water
* measuring tape

The water dripping or running out of melting glaciers is not clean and clear. It is full of dirt, sand, and rocks. How far do the dirt, sand, and rocks travel? Which goes the farthest? Does it make a difference if the water is moving fast or slow? What happens if the water stops, then starts again later?

1 Label a new page in your journal "Glacier Gush." Read all the steps, then set up a scientific method worksheet and complete as much of it as you can.

2 Cover the bottom of the bucket with sand, small pebbles, and rocks. Add water until the bucket is more than half full.

3 Go outside to a small hill covered with grass, concrete, or dirt. Predict which way the water will go when you dump it out. Write your prediction in your journal.

4 Swirl the bucket around a few times and then count to 10 as you slowly pour it out.

5 What do you see? Sketch your observations in your journal. Use the measuring tape to determine how far each material traveled (water, sand, small pebbles, rocks). Record your data.

TRY THIS! Try this experiment again at the same place to see if it moves the earlier materials. Do one on a hill with a different land covering. What happens differently?

PROJECT!

CANDY BAR CORE

Every time glaciers in an ice age melt, their meltwater carries a lot of rocks, dirt, and sand down the rivers toward to ocean. Since there have been more than 20 ice ages, a lot of layers have piled up!

Sometimes, scientists can see all the layers. They might be uncovered by weather events or by big earth-moving machines digging into the ground. In some places, where they know there are many bones, paleontologists dig carefully, looking for everything from big bones to tiny grains of pollen.

It would be difficult to do a dig at the bottom of the ocean. To study the layers there, geologists take a core sample. They push a tube down through the layers. When they bring the tube back up, they study each layer. In this project, you'll create your own core sample from a candy bar.

> **1** Label a new page in your journal, "Candy Bar Core." Read all the steps, then set up a scientific method worksheet and complete as much of it as you can.

2 Unwrap a candy bar. Put the clear straw over a place near the middle. Push down as hard as you can. Try not to break or bend the straw.

SUPPLIES

* Ice Age journal
* colored pencils
* several snack-size candy bars with multiple layers, such as Snickers, Milky Way, Butterfinger
* clear straw

WORDS ᴛᴏ KNOW

pollen: a fine, yellow powder produced by flowering plants. Pollen is spread around by the wind, birds, and **insects**, and is needed by a flower to reproduce.

insect: an animal that has three body parts and six legs and its skeleton on the outside of its body. Many insects have wings. Grasshoppers, ants, ladybugs, and honeybees are all insects.

core sample: when a tube-like drill is pushed into the earth to bring back a small part of what is underground, in the original layers.

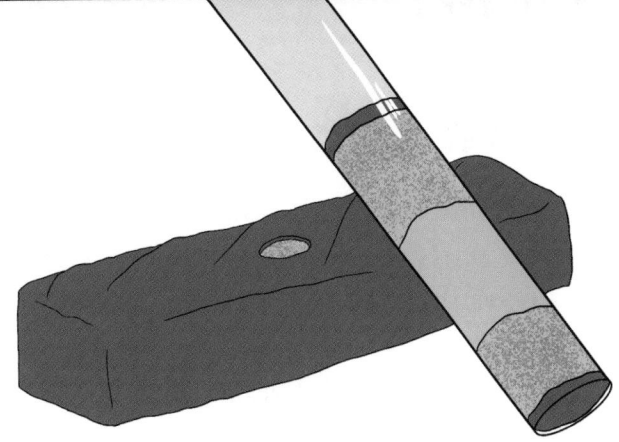

PROJECT!

3 Lift the straw up and out of the candy bar. What do you observe? Use your colored pencils to sketch and label the layers. Match the layers of candy to the layers of soil in the chart.

4 Do you find any colors or textures that repeat? How would that happen in nature? Which layer would be the oldest in a real core sample? Sketch your observations in your journal.

TRY THIS! Compare core samples from different places in the same candy bar. Do they all look exactly the same? What does that tell you about sampling?

Common layers found in candy bar cores	
Soft brown layer	muddy sea bed
Brown or orange crumbly layer	sand
Hard, roundish chunks (nuts)	big rocks moved by glaciers
Small, brittle pieces (rice)	animal bones
White, flexible strands (coconut)	plant stems or branches
Soft, light-colored layer	dirt
Sticky soft layer	tar

PROJECT!

DATING GAME

SUPPLIES

* Ice Age journal
* pencil
* fresh popcorn kernels
* measuring spoons
* plate
* soft (but not melted) butter or margarine
* 3 paper bags
* microwave
* timer

The bodies of plants and animals change after they die. Some parts rot away completely. Other parts change in ways that you might not be able to see, but that scientists can measure. Scientists tell the age of once-living things by looking at what is left in long-dead plants and animals.

Imagine the bones of all living things had popcorn kernels in them. After an animal or plant died and the body got older, some of the kernels popped. As time passed, more and more kernels would pop. Scientists could tell how old a bone was by comparing the number of popped and unpopped kernels.

1 Label a new page in your Ice Age journal "Dating Game." Read all the steps, then set up a scientific method worksheet and complete as much of it as you can.

2 On your plate, make three piles of popcorn kernels. Each pile should have 2 tablespoons of kernels.

3 Mix 1 teaspoon butter into each pile and form the mixture into the shape of a bone. Sketch all three of your "bones" in your Ice Age journal.

4 Label each paper bag as follows: A, 30 seconds; B, 60 seconds; C, 90 seconds. Put one bone in each bag. Imagine each second is 100 years. This means Bag A has a 3,000-year-old bone in it (30 x 100), Bag B has a 6,000-year-old bone in it (60 x 100), and Bag C has a 9,000-year-old bone in it (90 x 100)!

5 Put Bag A in the microwave. Set it on high for 2 minutes. As soon as you hear the first pop, set another timer for 30 seconds. Stop the microwave after those 30 seconds, even if it hasn't been a full 2 minutes. Carefully remove the bone. Sketch what you see. Count and record the number of both popped and unpopped kernels.

6 Put Bag B in the microwave. Set it on high for 2 minutes. As soon as you hear the first pop, time another 60 seconds. Carefully remove the bone. Sketch what you see. Count and record the number of kernels.

7 Put Bag C in the microwave and set it on high for 2 minutes. As soon as you hear the first pop, time another 90 seconds. Carefully remove the popcorn bone and sketch what you see. Count and record the number of kernels.

8 Make a graph to compare the differences between the three bones.

THINK ABOUT IT: If you were trying to estimate the age of these bones, which would be older? Which would be younger? How could you tell?

TAR PITS

SUPPLIES

* ❋ Ice Age journal
* ❋ pencil
* ❋ small pieces of sponge
* ❋ scissors
* ❋ plastic dish
* ❋ water
* ❋ salt
* ❋ corn syrup
* ❋ food coloring
* ❋ spoon
* ❋ waxed paper

At the La Brea Tar Pits in Los Angeles, California, animals were buried in thick, gooey tar. The flesh of the animals rotted away quickly. During a long period of time, the tar oozed into the tiny holes in the bones and hardened. The hardened tar stayed in the shape of the bone. It was a fossil.

1 Label a new page in your Ice Age journal, "Tar Pits." Read all the steps, then set up a scientific method worksheet and complete as much of it as you can.

2 Cut the pieces of sponge into bone or body part shapes, such as a heart. Make two of each shape so you can compare them.

THE LA BREA TAR PITS
CREDIT: BETSY WEBER

3 In the plastic dish, mix together 4 tablespoons hot tap water, 1 tablespoon salt, 2 tablespoons corn syrup, and 2 drops each of red, blue, and green food coloring. This is your tar pit.

4 Place one of each pair of sponge pieces on top of your tar pit. Watch for 3 minutes and record your observations. Choose below, the fast version or the slow version.

Fast version: After the sponge bones have been in the tar pit for at least 10 minutes, use the spoon to scoop them out. Place on the waxed paper so they are not touching each other. Put them in a sunny, dry place and examine them after they are dry.

Slow version: Place the tar pit in a warm, sunny location. Check on it every day. You will notice that a thin, harder layer will form on top. This is similar to the tar pits. If you break this film, you will notice the liquid is getting gooier. If you break the top coat every day, the tar pit will dry out faster.

5 Excavate your bones when dry. Compare the weight of the sponge pieces from the tar pit and those that were not in the tar pit. Are they different? What do you notice about the color and weight of the bones that were in your tar pit?

TRY THIS: Real fossils can break, but they won't dissolve in water. Test your fossil models. Can they break? What happens if you spray water on them or leave them in a tub of water? If you were estimating the age of these bones, which would be older? Which would be younger? How could you tell?

MY PRESENT PAST

SUPPLIES

* Ice Age journal
* pencil
* highlighter marker

During the Ice Age, people didn't have garbage cans. Piles of rock chips where people made tools stayed right where they were left. Broken spears were left at hunt sites. Spear points remained in bones. These remains give us clues about how people lived so long ago. What clues do you leave behind that people could study in 10,000 years?

1 Label a new page in your Ice Age journal, "My Present Past." For one day, write down everything you use or touch. Start with your bed and everything on it. Include your house, yard, and everything else.

2 Look carefully at each item. Those things that are made from plants (cloth, wood, some foods) or animals (fur, leather, some foods) would probably be eaten or rotted away in 10,000 years. Use the marker to highlight those things made of metal, rock, plastic, glass, or other permanent material.

3 Pick two highlighted items. Draw and describe each one in your journal. Do you think people in 10,000 years will know what those items are? Be creative and think of some other ways they might think you could have used them.

THINK ABOUT IT: Can you see why people thought this skull was from a one-eyed monster instead of a mammoth?

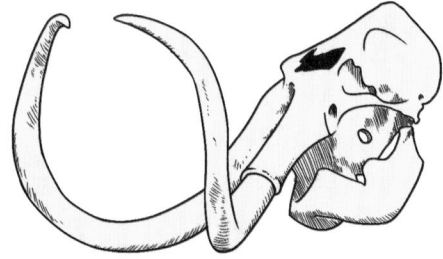

CHAPTER 3

MAMMOTHS AND MORE

During the Ice Age, there were animals large and small, familiar and strange, all around the world. If you lived back then, you might see hawks, owls, geese, giant mammoths, bison, giant sloths, and armored glyptodonts!

You might also see horses, camels, saber-toothed cats, foxes, deer, and badgers. And many of the animals that you are familiar with might have looked much different!

? INVESTIGATE!

How have the animals around you adapted to survive?

habitat: the natural area where a plant or animal lives.

adaptation: something about a plant or animal that helps it survive in its habitat.

WORDS ⊙ KNOW

All of these animals were able to survive Ice Age **habitats** because of certain **adaptations**.

For those animals that lived near the glaciers all year, it helped to have thick skin. Some woolly mammoths had skin that was 1 inch thick! These hardy animals also put on a heavy layer of fat. The fat kept them warm and provided energy when it was hard to find food.

Most of the animals living near glaciers had at least two layers of fur. The fur closest to the skin was short and very thick. This fur insulated the skin and didn't let water get near it. The outer fur often had very long hairs that shed rain and snow.

herbivore: an animal that eats only plants.

WORDS TO KNOW

WHAT DO YOU CALL A CAT ON ICE?

HA HA HA!

One cool cat.

Another big plus was to have big feet! Big feet act like snowshoes, making it easier to walk on top of snow and ice.

Thick, heavy, and big are good words for describing some of the best-known Ice Age animals. Picture the woolly mammoth, saber-toothed cats, short-faced bears, and giant deer. How could being big help them?

ANIMALS THAT FOLLOW THE FOOD

During the Ice Age summers, the plants growing near glaciers grew fast and tall. For the large flocks of ducks, geese, and songbirds, and herds of elk, deer, and other herbivores, it was the perfect habitat. The lush plants, swarming insects, and wide, open spaces were just the right setting to have a family.

ICE WORMS!

Many animals have adapted to survive near glaciers, but what about an animal that can survive only on a glacier? Meet the ice worm! These creatures look like miniature earthworms, but they hate the sun and spend their lives in and on the ice.

PS

You can watch a video and see photographs of ice worms here.

KEYWORD PROMPTS

glacier ice worm video

carnivore: an animal that eats meat.

migrate: to move from one habitat to another according to the season.

WORDS TO KNOW

Right alongside these animals were the carnivores. The meat-eating wolves, lions, jaguars, eagles, and hawks needed the plant-eating animals for food.

When the weather started to get cold in the fall, the plants and insects would die. The animals that could not survive a cold winter migrated away from the glaciers to warmer areas. It was more crowded in these warm areas and there was more competition for food there. So when the season changed and northern areas got warmer again, these animals migrated back to the glaciers.

HUMAN'S FIRST BEST FRIEND

Paleontologists and archaeologists believe that wild gray wolves started hanging around humans sometime during the Ice Age. They might have been eating leftovers and food trash that people didn't want. Or maybe humans found some pups and raised them. Scientists are hoping the mummies of two Ice Age puppies found in Siberia in 2011 will give them some clues about dogs and their relationship with humans.

Groups of humans migrated along with the animals. People hunted the animals for their meat, fur, and bones. They collected the long hairs to braid into ropes and weave into cloth. They even collected dried animal droppings to use as fuel for their fires.

mammal: an animal such as a human, dog, or cat. Mammals are born live, feed milk to their young, and usually have hair or fur covering most of their skin.

hibernate: to spend a period of time completely inactive in order to survive harsh conditions.

WORDS TO KNOW

SNOOZING THROUGH WINTER

Some mammals survive the winter by hibernating. Hibernation is when an animal is inactive for a long period of time in order to survive.

When an animal is hibernating, it takes fewer breaths each minute. Its heart beats much slower. Its body temperature drops, sometimes to nearly freezing. It doesn't wake up to eat, drink, or even go to the bathroom! Animals that hibernate eat as much as they can during the warmer months to get really fat. Their bodies use the fat as food energy while they sleep.

Cave bears and the Arctic ground squirrel were two Ice Age mammals that survived the winter by hibernating. Can you think of animals that hibernate today?

• DID YOU KNOW? • • • • • • • • • • • • • •

While hibernating, the Arctic ground squirrel's body temperature drops to about 27 degrees Fahrenheit (-2.9 degrees Celsius). That is below the freezing temperature of water!

reptile: an animal covered with scales that moves on its belly or on short legs. A snake, turtle, lizard, and alligator are all reptiles.

amphibian: an animal, such as a frog, toad, or salamander, that is usually born in the water but can spend time on land. They do not have scales or fur covering their skin.

WORDS TO KNOW

DID YOU KNOW?

Plenty of fish, reptiles, amphibians, spiders, and insects lived during the Ice Age. These animals were an important source of food for some of the bigger, better-known animals.

WHERE DID THE ICE AGE ANIMALS GO?

When Earth started warming up around 20,000 years ago, the glaciers started to melt. The warmer weather allowed more trees and larger plants to grow in new areas. For large Ice Age animals that needed grasses and flowers to eat, there was less food, because the larger plants crowded out the smaller food plants.

MOVIE FACT CHECK

Scrat, the saber-toothed squirrel from the *Ice Age* movies, started out as an imaginary animal. In 2005, paleontologists were surprised when they found the skull of a real saber-toothed mammal that would have looked like a squirrel and been about the same size. They had never seen an animal like that before. However, the real saber-toothed squirrel lived during the time of dinosaurs, more than 100 million years ago. There were none left by the time of the ice ages.

At the same time, humans were inventing better tools and becoming better hunters. They were able to kill more of the large animals. All the woolly mammoths, woolly rhinoceroses, giant sloths, cave bears, short-faced bears, saber-toothed cats, and many others died. They are now extinct.

Some Ice Age animals, such as beavers and sloths, became smaller through time. Ice Age animals that are still around today include moose, grizzly bears, musk oxen, caribou, picas, and Arctic ground squirrels. Apes, deer, rabbits, kangaroos, camels, and jaguars are animals that lived far from glaciers during the Ice Age and are still alive today.

And, of course, there are still humans! How have humans changed since the Ice Age? We'll take a look in the next chapter.

? CONSIDER AND DISCUSS

It's time to consider and discuss: How have the animals around you adapted to survive?

PROJECT!

SIZE ME UP!

Ice Age mammoths, giant sloths, short-faced bears, and camels were much bigger than their living relatives are today. Use these measurements to draw life-sized sketches of an Ice Age mammoth!

Mammoth:

- Height: 10 feet at shoulder

- Length: 14 feet (not including tusks)

- Tusks: about 8 feet long

1 Put a piece of graph paper in your journal and label it "Size Me Up." You can find graph paper online to print.

KEYWORD PROMPTS

print graph paper 🔍

2 Imagine each square of your graph paper is 1 foot in length. Use your pencil to mark the squares that would be at the edges of the mammoth. This will help you outline a mammoth that is close to the right size. Use the picture on the next page as a guide.

3 Go outside to a large, flat, paved driveway or parking lot. You will be drawing a giant chalk grid. This will help you draw the animal the right size. Stretch out your measuring tape. Use the chalk to make a small X at every foot. Make this line at least 20 feet long.

SUPPLIES

✳ Ice Age journal

✳ graph paper with ½ inch grid

✳ pencil

✳ measuring tape

✳ sidewalk chalk

✳ large paved driveway or parking lot

✳ camera (optional)

4 At one end of this line, stretch your measuring tape so it makes a sharp corner, or a 90-degree angle. Use the chalk to make a small X at every foot. Make this line at least 20 feet long.

5 Move the measuring tape to the other end of the first line and repeat your measuring and marking. Then move the measuring tape so it stretches between the top end of the two lines. Repeat your measuring and marking.

6 Use the measuring tape to connect the small X's from top to bottom and side to side. It should look like a giant grid.

7 Use the picture on the graph paper in your journal as your guide to drawing a life-size mammoth.

8 Take a picture of yourself lying in or next to the outlines.

TRY THIS! Look in books or magazines for pictures of Ice Age animals that you want to draw. Research the actual size of each animal, then draw them to scale.

POUNDS OF PRESSURE

The bigger an animal's feet, the easier it is for the animal to walk on snow or spongy summer tundra ground without sinking in. These and other adaptations help determine where different animals can live.

How big were mammoth feet? Scientists have noticed that the distance around the edge of modern elephant feet is about half the animal's shoulder height. If the same was true for a woolly mammoth with a shoulder 10 feet tall, its foot would be about 5 feet around! This might be bigger than you!

SUPPLIES

* Ice Age journal
* pencil
* round cake pan
* flour
* empty small plastic cup such as a yogurt cup or laundry detergent cup
* salt, nails, metal washers, rocks, or other heavy items
* small plastic plate (smaller than your cake pan)
* ruler

1 Label a new page in your journal, "Pounds of Pressure." Read all the steps, then set up a scientific method worksheet and complete as much of it as you can.

2 Fill the cake pan almost full with flour. Shake it gently side-to-side to make it level across the top.

3 Fill the small plastic cup with nails or other the heavy items. These are your weights.

4 Gently place the cup in the middle of the flour-filled pan. Do not push down! Let it sit for 10 seconds.

5 Carefully remove the cup. Use the ruler to measure how deep an impression (if any) the cup made in the flour.

6 Move the weights from the cup to the plastic plate. Be sure to scatter the weights evenly around the plate.

7 Gently shake the pan of flour side to side to create a level surface. Place the plate on top of the flour. Do not push down. Let it sit for 10 seconds.

8 Carefully remove the plate. Use the ruler to measure how deep an impression (if any) the plate made in the flour.

THINK ABOUT IT: Which sunk in more, the cup or the plate? Why? What does this mean for animals with small feet trying to walk on snow?

PROJECT!

MAKING TRACKS

SUPPLIES

* Ice Age journal
* pencil
* measuring tape
* chalk

You can learn a lot about an animal just by looking at its tracks. Short-faced bears made flat-footed tracks that pointed straight ahead. Bears today make pigeon-toed tracks with feet that slide in. Based on these observations, some paleontologists believe short-faced bears were much faster runners than bears are today. What can you learn by investigating the feet and tracks of your family and friends?

1 Label a new page in your journal, "Making Tracks." Make a chart like the one below.

Name	Age	Height	Foot length	Leg length	Walking stride # of steps/20 feet	Running stride # of steps/20 feet

PROJECT!

2 Use the measuring tape to measure the height, foot length, and leg length of each person. Record the numbers in the chart.

3 Stride is the distance between an animal's feet when it is moving. Use the chalk and measuring tape to mark two lines 20 feet apart on a sidewalk, driveway, or parking lot.

4 Have each person walk between the two lines, counting how many normal steps they take.

5 To find the walking stride, divide 20 feet by the number of steps they took.

6 Have each person run between the two lines, counting how many steps they take.

7 To find the running stride, divide 20 feet by the number of running steps they took.

8 Compare your numbers. Do taller people have bigger feet? Do people with bigger feet take longer strides?

TRY THIS! Compare the foot size of parents and their kids. Can you estimate how big someone will grow to be by the size of their feet?

BUNDLED BOTTLES

How can you stay warm if you go outside on a cold day? Bundle up! Putting on more clothes helps keep you warm. Wild animals can't put on more clothes, but they do grow thicker layers of fat and fur to keep themselves warmer.

SUPPLIES

* 3 zippered plastic bags big enough to hold one water bottle
* solid vegetable shortening
* spoon
* wool sock
* 2 small plastic water bottles with lids
* water
* Ice Age journal
* pencil
* thermometer

1 Put three big spoonfuls of shortening in one plastic bag. Turn another plastic bag inside out. Push it into the bag with the shortening and zipper the two bags together. Use your hands to spread the shortening out so it makes an even layer between the bags.

2 Place the bag inside the sock. The sock is the base layer of an animal's fur. The bags are like the skin of an animal. The shortening is the extra fat that animals get before winter.

3 Use warm tap water to fill each bottle. Measure and record the temperature of the water in each bottle.

4 Place one bottle in the double bag with the layer of shortening. Close the other bottle inside the plain zippered bag. Place both bottles side by side in the freezer.

5 How long do you think it will take for each to freeze? Remove the bottles each hour to check and record the temperatures of the water. What happens? Which bottle freezes first?

TRY THIS! Repeat the project using one large water bottle and one small water bottle. What do you observe?

PROJECT!

ANTIFREEZE

Some animals, including fish, turtles, frogs, insects, spiders, and worms, don't have fur. How did they survive living near the glaciers? By using a natural antifreeze. Some animals today can do the same thing.

SUPPLIES

* 2 small plastic containers with tight lids, such as yogurt cups
* masking tape
* markers
* sugar
* spoon
* water
* 2 zippered plastic baggies
* Ice Age journal
* pencil

1 Place a piece of tape on the lid of each container. Label one, "Container A." Label the other, "Container B."

2 Pour two spoonfuls of sugar into Container A. Add warm water and stir until the sugar is dissolved. Pour more water into the container to the very top and put on the lid. Fill Container B to the top with water. Put on the lid.

3 Put each container in its own plastic baggie. Zipper each baggie shut. Place both containers in a freezer. Make sure they are standing upright.

4 Start a scientific method worksheet in your Ice Age journal. Check on the containers at least once a day. What happens? Record your observations in your journal.

TRY THIS! Experiment to discover the least amount of sugar you need to keep your animal from freezing.

CHAPTER 4

PALEO PEOPLE

If you were alive during the Ice Age, what would you need to survive? The same basic things you need today—shelter, warmth, water, and food. But you couldn't go to a store or have things delivered to you. If you lived during the Ice Age, you and your friends would have to find, catch, or make everything you needed.

For example, where would you sleep? How would you stay warm? What would you wear? What would you eat, how would you cook your food, and how would you make sure you had enough water to drink?

INVESTIGATE!

What would life be like if you had to make everything you use instead of buying it?

FINDING SHELTER

Maybe you would make your home in a cave. But not all parts of the world have caves. And many caves are too small, too cold, too wet, or too dangerous. A cave might already be home to wild animals, including bats and bears.

However, archaeologists and anthropologists have found evidence that some Ice Age people did live in caves, at least part of the time. In Europe, scientists have found rock fire rings, stone tools, animal bones, bone tools, beads made from teeth, and paintings in caves.

People who lived in caves probably didn't stay there all year. In the summer, the land near the glaciers would warm up a bit and lots of plants would grow very fast. People could eat some of these plants. They could also hunt the large herbivores, including mammoths and reindeer, that came to feed on the plants. Not only did they eat the meat, they used all other parts of their catch, too, including the hair, skin, and bones.

Since people needed these animals for so many things, they followed the migrating herds. However, the people couldn't take their caves with them. Scientists believe they made tents out of animal bones and skins for shelter.

MOVIE FACT CHECK

The human family in the movie *Ice Age* had to move their camp when winter was coming. This was true in real life as well!

Scientists have found signs that some people built houses. The houses might have been summer shelters close to the glacier. Some anthropologists now believe that people lived near the glaciers all year round! If you lived near the glaciers, you would need a sturdy shelter.

Near the glaciers, there were no trees that could be used to build houses or fires. But there were mammoth bones, and these were big and sturdy. Humans realized they could use those bones to frame a shelter. Big animal skins put over the bones and held in place with rocks or other bones made a house. Some of these houses used more than 400 bones!

PS Take a virtual tour of a recreated mammoth bone hut here!

KEYWORD PROMPTS

Mezhirich Ukraine mammoth bone hut

KEEPING WARM

Caves, mammoth bone houses, and simple tents could help people stay out of bad weather and safe from some animals. But people needed more to stay warm. One great way to keep warm is to be near a fire.

flint: a very hard, grayish-black rock.

pyrite: a shiny yellow mineral used to start a fire.

mineral: a naturally occurring solid found in rocks and in the ground. Rocks are made of minerals. Gold and diamonds are precious minerals.

WORDS ⊕ KNOW

Ice Age people used fire to keep warm and cook food. Fire could also be used to heat rocks, bones, and sticks to make into tools. And fire kept away wild animals that might attack people or steal their food.

Some anthropologists think people used fires that were first started by lightning. Then they could carry around hot coals in animal horns. When they needed a new fire, they would put dry moss, animal hair, or small sticks in a pile and add a coal.

Other anthropologists think that Ice Age people knew how to start fires. Of course, they didn't have matches! But you don't need matches to start a fire. People can make sparks by striking flint and pyrite rocks together. Some of these rocks and minerals have been found near Ice Age homes and camps.

poncho: a cape that falls in the back and the front with a hole for the head.

sinew: a strong band of animal tissue that connects muscle to bone.

WORDS TO KNOW

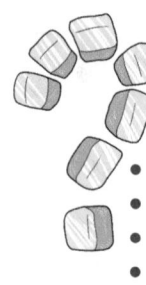

· DID YOU KNOW? · · · ·

How can you tell if a rock was part of a fire ring? When a rock is next to fire, the heat of the fire can change the color and hardness of a rock.

How can you keep warm if you aren't near fire? Clothes! People invented stone tools to scrape the meat off the skin of animal pelts. Then, it was easy to use the furry animal hide as a warm blanket, rug, or cape. Ice Age people dried the skins and softened them to make leather. They even used stone tools to cut holes in the leather to make a poncho.

At some time during the Ice Age, people thought of putting two pieces of animal skin together. They poked holes in each piece of skin. A piece of string made from animal hair, sinew, or braided grass stems could be pushed or pulled through each hole.

This took a lot of time—what if there were a tool that could poke a hole and pull a string at the same time? It probably took a lot of tries, but eventually people were using needles made from thin slivers of bones, antlers, and tusks. The sewing needle is one of the oldest inventions that modern people are still using!

WHAT DID THE BIG FURRY HAT SAY TO THE WARM WOOLLY SCARF?

HA HA HA!

You hang around while I go on ahead.

FINDING FOOD

Scientists think our first foods were mostly plants. If you know where and when to look, it can be pretty easy to find berries, nuts, roots, and even plant stems that are good to eat. Early humans might also have eaten meat from animals that were already dead or killed by other animals, but they needed more dining options.

Ice Age people were surrounded by nature. They watched rocks fall and break. Maybe someone fell on a rock and cut their skin. This might have given them ideas for how to cut the skin of animals.

ICE AGE CLOTHING

We have very limited evidence about the clothes Ice Age people made and wore. Most of their clothes rotted away. Archaeologists get some clues from the placement of bone, shell, and teeth decorations found on bodies in graves. They are also getting clues from carved statues that may show clothes. On some of these statues, there are imprints of woven cloth patterns. These may show that people were weaving plant stems or animal hairs to make cloth.

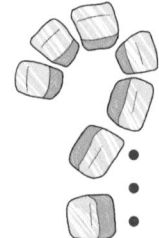

DID YOU KNOW?

Knappers are people who make tools out of rocks. Archaeologists have found that flint, chert, obsidian, and quartz were used quite often by ancient knappers. These tool makers made sharp knives, spear points, and thin rock drills that could etch bones or stones.

At some point, people started breaking certain rocks on purpose. After using rocks to skin animals and cut meat, someone might have had the idea to use a sharp, pointed rock to kill an animal.

Later, people started attaching sharp rocks to sticks to make hunting spears. The first spears were likely used to jab animals from a short distance. But it is much safer to hunt a big animal if you don't have to stand right next to it! Eventually, people invented spears they could throw.

Do you think you could have survived in the Ice Age? Humans might feel that the Ice Age is gone for good, but scientists tell us that our climate is changing. We'll learn more about the possibility for another ice age in the next chapter!

 **CONSIDER AND DISCUSS**

It's time to consider and discuss: What would life be like if you had to make everything you use instead of buying it?

SAVE THE GRAVES

For many years, archaeologists and treasure hunters liked to dig up ancient burial sites. Some people pointed out that it wasn't respectful to disturb graves on purpose. Laws were passed to protect these places. Now, if a human burial site is uncovered, people work to preserve it or move the contents to a safer place.

ELEMENTARY ETCHINGS

Ice Age people left behind many images of things that were important to them. They used sharp, pointed sticks, rocks, and bone pieces to scratch designs on cave walls, bones, antlers, and rocks. This is called etching. You can try your hand at etching on a much easier surface—your journal cover! Remember, once you start your etching, you can't erase any mistakes.

SUPPLIES

* ✳ Ice Age journal
* ✳ paper
* ✳ chalk (optional)
* ✳ etching tool— pencil, skewer, or round toothpick

1 Plan what you want to etch. You can make a few sketches first on scrap paper. If you want to make an outline to follow, draw your plan with chalk on your journal cover.

2 Place your journal cover on a flat surface. Gently press the pointed tip of your etching tool into the surface of the cover. Be careful not to press it all the way through! Slowly move the tool. You might want to create a light groove first, and then deepen it by going over it a second time. It helps to lift your hand from the surface a few times as you go.

TRY THIS! Some etchings made by Paleolithic artists are easier to see when a rubbing is made of them. Place a piece of copy paper over your etching. Gently rub the side of your pencil lead back and forth over the surface. Watch your drawing appear on the paper!

WORDS ⊙ KNOW

etching: to make a drawing by using a sharp tool to dig lines into a hard surface.

MAKE A PONCHO

SUPPLIES

* 4 large brown paper bags
* scissors
* string or twine
* hole punch
* needle
* Ice Age journal
* pencil

Animal skin gets very stiff as it dries. Ice Age people knew they had to work the skin to make it soft and easy to wear. Some scientists believe the women may have even chewed the animal skins to make them soft. For this project, don't put your material in your mouth! Find other ways of making it soft.

1 Imagine each bag is the skin of an animal. Your first job is to cut the skin. Use your scissors to cut up through the middle of one wide side of one bag. Cut a big circle in the bottom of this bag for your neck.

2 To soften each skin, crumple the bag into a tight ball. Smooth it out, and then crumple it again. Do this several times. Be careful not to tear it.

3 Model one bag as a cape. Simply put it over your shoulders. Try to play ball or turn a cartwheel. What happens to your cape? How could you improve its design? Sketch your cape and record your observations in your Ice Age journal.

4 Try making a poncho. Fold another bag flat. Use your scissors to cut just the bottom off the bag. Open the bag and pull it over your head. Sketch your poncho and record your observations in your journal. How can you improve the design?

5 How about a fitted coat? Cut one bag like a cape. Then cut arm holes about 2 inches down from each narrow side on the bottom. Punch holes around the entire edge of each armhole.

6 Your fourth bag will be used to make sleeves for the coat. Cut the bottom off the bag like you were making a poncho. Cut down opposite seams on the sides to make two wide panels. Use the hole punch to make a line of holes along each side of each panel.

7 Cut a long piece of string. Curl each panel into a tube shape and line up the holes. Push the string through two holes near one end and tie a knot. Take the free end of the string and push it through the line of holes to sew them together.

8 When you get to the top of the sleeve, do not cut the string. Use it to sew the sleeve onto an armhole.

9 Repeat steps 7 and 8 for the other sleeve. Then try on your coat!

THINK ABOUT IT: Write your observations about how much work it takes to make each type of covering. Which one stays on the best? Which one allows you to run around and throw a ball best? Which one keeps you warmest and driest?

WEAVE A BELT

SUPPLIES

* ✳ ball of yarn or string
* ✳ scissors

Some archaeologists believe that Ice Age people wove plant stalks or long animal hairs to make fabrics. These fabrics could have been used to make clothes and bags. What do you need to weave a narrow scarf or belt? Some string or yarn and your fingers!

1 Pull out a long piece of yarn or string from the ball, but do not cut it.

2 Pinch the loose end between your thumb and palm on one hand or tie it around your thumb.

3 Start the yarn on the outside edge of your pointer finger. Go behind the pointer finger then loosely between each other finger across to your little finger and back again. There should be a single strand across the front and back of each finger.

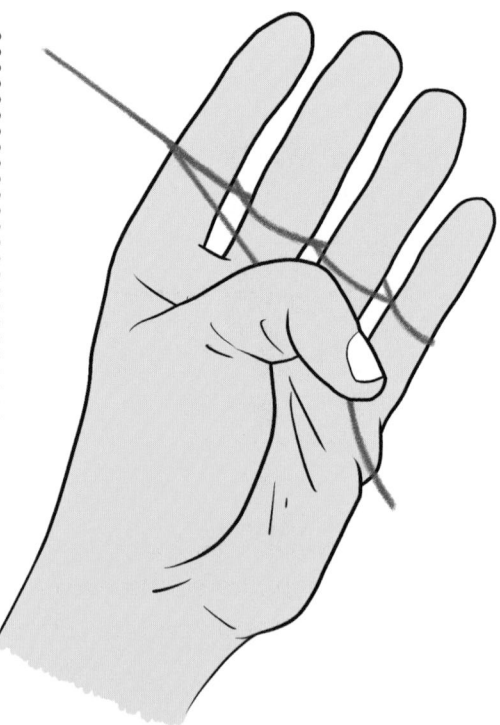

4 After ending by your pointer finger, wrap the yarn all the way across the back of your fingers, and then straight across the front of your fingers above the loops. Do not pull it tight.

5 Hold your hand flat with your palm facing up so the yarn hangs down by your pointer finger.

6 Use your other hand to move the strand at the base of each finger over the other strand and over the top of your finger. You will have to bend each finger as you do this.

7 Repeat laying a single strand across the back then front of your fingers, then lifting the loops over to create a woven chain.

8 After a few rounds, you can let go of the piece under your thumb. When your weaving gets as long as you want it to be, cut the unused yarn a few inches from your hand. Weave that free end of yarn through the strand at the bottom of each finger and cinch it tight to make a knot.

TRY THIS! Experiment by using several yarns at the same time, switching colors to make patterns, and combining the chains to make wider pieces.

PROJECT!

SPRAY PAINT

SUPPLIES

✳ drinking straw
✳ full cup of water
✳ scissors
✳ food coloring
✳ copy paper
✳ tape
✳ leaf or other object to spray

Ice Age artists had only four colors to work with: red, yellow, brown, and black. They made the colors by using crushed-up minerals or charcoal. For some paintings, they dabbed on the colors using brushes made of pine needles or wads of animal fur. Outlines of their hands were made by spray painting! You can do this, too, but it is best done outside or some other place that can get wet!

1 About 2 inches from one end of the straw, make a cut that goes almost all the way across.

2 Bend the small piece down and put it in the water next to the edge of the cup. Be sure to keep the slit above the water!

3 Point the cut edge of the straw toward a flower, plant, wall, or some other target.

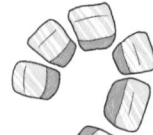

• DID YOU KNOW? • • • • • •

Many cave paintings are found deep inside caves, in parts where people did not usually live. This makes many anthropologists believe the paintings were made as part of special ceremonies.

WORDS TO KNOW

charcoal: the dark carbon pieces that remain after wood and other materials are burned.

68

PROJECT!

4 Put your lips around the end of the long section of the straw. Blow hard! The moving air will pull water up from the cup. The spray will fly toward your target. Practice standing different distances away to see which one works best for you.

5 After practicing a few times, you are ready make a spray paint print. Add a few drops of coloring to your water and stir. Tape a piece of paper to an outdoor wall. Loop one or two pieces of tape under the leaf and stick it to the paper. Stand back and spray away!

6 After the spray paint has dried, remove the leaf. Tape this sheet to the inside cover of your journal.

TRY THIS! Experiment with straws of different sizes with the slits cut at different lengths. Which straw works the best for you?

LOVE THOSE LEVERS!

SUPPLIES

* Ice Age journal
* pencil
* masking tape
* bag of marshmallows
* measuring tape
* small spoon
* big spoon
* soup ladle

Levers are simple tools that increase the amount of force you have. Have you ever used a see-saw, baseball bat, or wheelbarrow? These are levers! Ice Age people invented tools that were levers that helped them become better hunters. They shaped sticks, antlers, and bones into spear throwers. Placing the butt of a spear on the tip of a thrower, they likely held the thrower over a shoulder and flicked the spear toward their targeted animal.

1 Draw a chart like the one below in your journal.

Launcher	Distance 1	Distance 2	Distance 3	Distance 4	Distance 5
Arm					
Small spoon					
Big spoon					
Soup ladle					
Other					

PROJECT!

2 Go outside and use the masking tape to make a start line on the ground.

3 Stand at the start line and throw five marshmallows, one at a time, as far as you can.

4 Use the measuring tape to record the distance of each throw. Pick up the marshmallows.

5 Repeat the throws, this time putting one marshmallow at a time in the bowl end of the small spoon. Measure and record the distance of each throw.

6 Repeat the marshmallow throws using the large spoon, then the ladle. Measure and record the distance of each throw.

7 Which spoon helped you throw the farthest? What other marshmallow thrower can you invent?

TRY THIS! Set your marshmallows out on a table for a few days to dry out. Does having harder marshmallows make a difference? Draw a target on a big box and test your aim. It can take some practice to become good at chucking marshmallows!

CHAPTER 5

ICE AGE AGAIN?

What would it be like to live during an Ice Age? Most scientists agree we are probably thousands of years away from the next natural ice age. But it is interesting to think about how it might happen and what it will be like.

Even if Earth was on the far edge of its cycle around the sun, the temperature would drop only a tiny bit. It takes a long, long time for it to get cold enough for an ice age to happen.

? INVESTIGATE!

Is there a best temperature for life on Earth?

Our atmosphere has been warming up. Humans have been creating more and more carbon dioxide that gets released into the atmosphere. This gas acts like a blanket and makes Earth warmer. Scientists are recording temperatures that are hotter than usual all around the world.

To help slow down the warming of Earth, some scientists are trying to bring back parts of the Ice Age. One theory is that by bringing back plants and animals that lived near the glaciers, we can help keep things cooler—but not enough to freeze the world!

WORDS TO KNOW

atmosphere: the blanket of gases around the earth.

carbon dioxide: a gas formed by the burning of **fossil fuels**, the rotting of plants and animals, and the breathing out of animals, including humans.

fossil fuel: a fuel made from the remains of plants and animals that lived millions of years ago. Coal, oil, and natural gas are fossil fuels.

WHY DID THE BOY GO TO SCHOOL WITH ONLY ONE GLOVE?

HA HA HA!

The weatherman said, "It's going to be cold, but on the other hand it might be warm."

MEET THE NENETS

There are still some people who live near glaciers. The Nenets in Siberia don't use stone tools or hunt mammoths, but they do live in warm tent shelters and follow migrating reindeer.

You can see photos of the Nenets here. How is their lifestyle different from yours?

KEYWORD PROMPTS

Nenets of Siberia video 🔍

A Russian scientist named Sergey Zimov started a nature reserve called Pleistocene Park in Siberia in 1977. In 1988, he and other scientists started raising reindeer, horses, moose, elk, bison, and musk oxen in a large fenced-in area. The hope is that these animals will help slow the thawing of the permafrost.

The animals will not be able to eat all the plants during the summer. When winter comes, there will be food under the snow. The animals will trample the snow and eat all the grass. This will uncover the ground and let the permafrost get nice and cold—so cold it will stay frozen longer in the summer. If their work is successful, other countries might start their own Pleistocene parks.

COME BACK, CRITTERS!

Of course, there are no extinct Ice Age animals in the park. At least, not yet! Scientists are working on ways to bring back large extinct animals, including the aurochs and the mammoth.

cross-breeding: mating two animals of the same type that are not exactly the same.

graze: to eat grass.

species: a group of living things that are closely related and produce young.

WORDS TO KNOW

The aurochs is the extinct Ice Age animal that might be the closest to a comeback. The last live aurochs that we know about lived in 1627. To bring it back, scientists in the Czech Republic are cross-breeding wild cows. Each type of cow they use has something in common with the ancient aurochs. It might be its color, size, grazing style, fur coat, or behavior. By 2025, scientists hope to have a new animal, called the Tauros, that is as close to the aurochs as they can get. Then, they hope to find places and parks where they can release these new-old animals and let them run wild!

Bringing back a mammoth is a much bigger job. Most mammoth species were extinct by about 10,000 years ago. There were a few populations of smaller mammoths on islands in the Arctic Ocean. These mammoths died out between 6,000 and 4,000 years ago.

DID YOU KNOW?

Ice Age scientists of all types know that the oldest rocks, fossils, bones, and tools are usually the ones deepest in the ground. The newest things, including modern trash, are closer to the surface.

DNA: the substance found in the cells of every living thing that determines everything about us: whether we are human, an insect, or something else, whether we have blue eyes or brown, are right- or left-handed, and every other trait that makes us who we are.

WORDS TO KNOW

Elephants are the closest relatives to mammoths, but no one thinks elephants could survive near a glacier. To bring back mammoths, scientists have to get bits of information, called DNA, from dead mammoth bodies. They might be able to use those bits of information to create a new mammoth. But there are a lot of challenges to figure out before this will work!

ICE AGE UP CLOSE

In Chapter 2, you learned that scientists still have a lot to learn about the Ice Age. Every clue they find gives them more information. Often, it's people just like you who find the clues, even kids!

Help scientists fit the clues together by paying attention to the land around you! Take a look at your landscape. Are there big rocks in strange places? Do farmers have rock piles or walls at the edges of their fields? Some of the best places to find bones and teeth are by creeks and streams. And check out the resources at the end of this book. There are places all around the country where you can see the Ice Age up close.

The world during the Ice Age was very different from the world today, and there's still a lot we can learn about how people and animals lived back then. Have fun discovering more about the Ice Age, and wear a coat!

CONSIDER AND DISCUSS

It's time to consider and discuss: Is there a best temperature for life on Earth?

MAMMOTH DINNERS

Mammoths were herbivores, eating only plants. For many years, scientists thought that mammoths and other plant eaters living near the ice fed mostly on grass. New research on frozen plants found in the tundra in Siberia might be changing that idea. One study has shown that a type of plantain might have been very common. Other studies have shown that plants related to buttercups, poppies, and other flowers grew on Ice Age tundra as well. There were some grasses, and in places that had enough water, small pine trees, willows, and spruces.

SUN STRETCH

One thing that affects our climate is how much the earth tilts as it orbits around the sun. Have you ever paid much attention to the cycle of the sun? One way to measure the tilt of the earth is to record how far sunshine stretches across your floor. This project is easy to do, but has the best results if you do it for a whole year!

SUPPLIES

* Ice Age journal
* pencil
* south-facing window
* tape measure
* masking tape (optional)
* camera

1 Start a scientific method worksheet in your journal. Pick a window that faces south and has plenty of open floor by it. On a cloudy day or at night, put one end of the tape measure on the floor by the bottom of the window. Stretch it out to make and record the following predictions:

* I think sunlight will stretch the farthest across the floor on _____ (date). I think it will go _____ (distance).

* I think sunlight will stay nearest to the window on _____ (date). I think it will go _____ (distance).

* Take pictures of the tape measure ending at both your predicted places. If you can, mark these spots with pieces of masking tape.

2 Make a chart like the one on the next page. The four dates listed are the start of spring, summer, fall, and winter. These are important days in the cycle of the sun. If the sun is not shining on those days, do your measuring on the next sunny day. Add as many other dates as you want.

PROJECT!

Date	Time	Distance from wall/bottom of window
March 21 Spring Equinox		
June 21 Summer Solstice		
September 21 Autumn Equinox		
December 21 Winter Solstice		

3 Try to make your measurements at the same time of day each time. The best time to measure is around noon, when the sun is highest in the sky. To measure the sun's reach, put one end of the measuring tape under the bottom of the window. Stretch it out to the far end of the sunlight. Take a picture and record its length.

4 Look at your results after six months. Look again after a year. What is the difference between your shortest and longest sun measurements? How close were your predictions? Do you notice a pattern?

THINK ABOUT IT: If there is some wall space between the window and the floor, the size of the shadow will also change. Use your observations to predict when the shadow will be the biggest and the smallest. Devise a way to test your predications.

BOTTLED EARTH

The earth is a bit like a giant terrarium. Gravity **holds our atmosphere in place. The gases trap some heat from the sun near the earth. The types of gases in the atmosphere and the thickness of the atmosphere play a role in how cold or warm the earth is. You can make and study two simple miniature models of the earth. They will help you compare and contrast how plants react to different conditions.**

Caution: Ask an adult to help you cut the bottles.

1 Label a new page in your journal "Bottled Earth." Read all the steps, then set up a scientific method worksheet and complete as much of it as you can.

2 Use the marker to draw a line around each bottle a little more than halfway up. Cut each bottle along the line. Ask an adult to help you.

3 Fill the bottom part of each bottle about half full with small rocks or pebbles.

4 Cut the mesh bath scrubby into two pieces. Place one piece in each bottle over the rocks. This will help keep the soil in place but will let water go through.

SUPPLIES

* Ice Age journal
* pencil
* permanent marker
* two 2-liter clear plastic bottles with caps
* scissors
* small rocks or pebbles
* mesh bath scrubby
* soil
* spoon
* seedlings from Chapter 1 or new seeds
* tablespoon
* water

WORDS TO KNOW

terrarium: a small enclosed habitat.

gravity: a force that pulls objects to the earth.

5 Spoon soil on top of the mesh pieces until it is almost to the top of the rim.

6 Place your seedlings or seeds in the soil. Be sure to cover any plant roots you have.

7 Slowly pour 2 to 3 tablespoons of water over the soil in each bottle. Most of the water will go down to the rocks.

8 Cut a small slit in one side of the top of each bottle. Place this over the plant bases, pushing down so it slides past the rims. Use the marker to label one bottle cap A and the other bottle cap B.

9 Put the bottles in a sunny window. Several times a week, open Bottle A and blow in several long breaths. You are adding carbon dioxide. Recap the bottle.

10 Look at your bottles several times a week and record your observations in your journal. Does adding carbon dioxide change the conditions of your plants? How?

TRY THIS! Place one bottle in a sunny window. Place the other bottle far away from a window (but not in a closet!). Record any differences you see.

MAMMOTH CODE

DNA tells our cells how to make our bodies. DNA has the code for the color of your hair, eyes, and skin, how tall you will grow, even whether you have dry or wet ear wax! DNA does this with only four main ingredients. The order of these four ingredients creates the code. When scientists try to get the code from ancient animals, it is often broken into small pieces. This makes it harder to know what the code would tell the cells to do.

SUPPLIES

* Ice Age journal
* pencil
* 2 by 1 Lego pieces, 20 each of 4 different colors
* 6 by 1 and 8 by 1 Lego pieces, different colors than the 2 by 1 pieces above
* permanent marker
* 2 paper bags

Caution: Ask permission before writing on Lego pieces with a permanent marker.

1 Label a new page in your journal "Mammoth Code." Read all the steps before completing as much of the scientific method as you can.

2 Sort the Lego pieces into piles by color. Use the marker to label the Legos. The colors should be A (adenine), T (thymine), C (cytosine), and G (guanine). These are the real names for the parts that make up the DNA code.

3 Connect each A with a T. Connect each C with a G. In nature, adenine and thymine always go together, as do cytosine and guanine.

PROJECT!

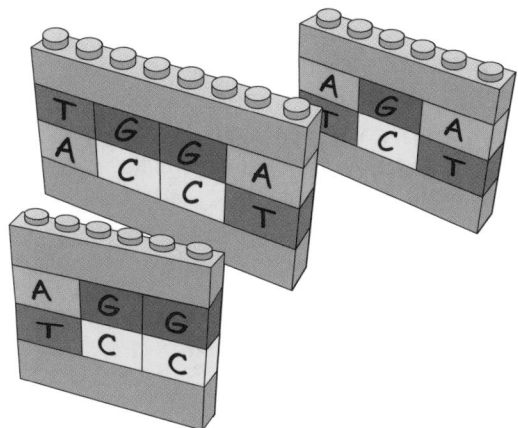

4 Make DNA stacks by putting code pieces on the longer skinny Legos.

5 Decide what each piece is a code for. Is one for eye color? How about foot size? Straight or curly hair? Record your codes in your journal.

6 Split DNA stacks down the middle so there are only single code pieces on each longer strand. Put each strand in a separate bag. Shake the bags hard. DNA gets broken up over time, and mammoths have been dead for a long time.

7 Imagine each bag is part of a mammoth mummy. One at a time, pull out one piece from one bag. Is it complete or broken? Can you match it with your code in your journal? Record all the information from one bag before starting on the other one.

8 How much information about your mammoth did you get from each bag?

TRY THIS! Leaving the single pieces alone, how much of the mammoth DNA can you put back together?

A

adaptation: something about a plant or animal that helps it survive in its habitat.

amphibian: an animal, such as a frog, toad, or salamander, that is usually born in the water but can spend time on land. They do not have scales or fur covering their skin.

artifact: an object made by people in the past, including tools, pottery, and jewelry.

atmosphere: the blanket of gases around the earth.

B

Beringia: the land between Siberia and Alaska that was exposed during the last ice age.

C

carbon dioxide: a gas formed by the burning of fossil fuels, the rotting of plants and animals, and the breathing out of animals, including humans.

carnivore: an animal that eats meat.

charcoal: the dark carbon pieces that remain after wood and other materials are burned.

climate: the average weather patterns in an area during a long period of time.

condense: when a gas cools down and changes into a liquid.

core sample: when a tube-like drill is pushed into the earth to bring back a small part of what is underground, in the original layers.

cross-breeding: mating two animals of the same type that are not exactly the same.

culture: the beliefs and way of life of a group of people.

cycle: a repeated series of events.

D

DNA: the substance found in the cells of every living thing that determines everything about us: whether we are human, an insect, or something else, whether we have blue eyes or brown, are right- or left-handed, and every other trait that makes us who we are.

E

equator: an imaginary line around the middle of the earth.

estimate: a best guess using facts you know.

etching: to make a drawing by using a sharp tool to dig lines into a hard surface.

evaporate: when a liquid heats up and changes into a gas, or vapor.

evidence: something that supports the existence of something or the truth of an idea.

extinct: when a group of plants or animals dies out and there are no more left in the world.

F

flint: a very hard, grayish-black rock.

force: a push or pull applied to an object that changes an object's motion.

fossil: the remains or traces of ancient life, including plants and animals.

fossil fuel: a fuel made from the remains of plants and animals that lived millions of years ago. Coal, oil, and natural gas are fossil fuels.

G

geology: the study of the earth and its rocks. A geologist studies geology.

glacier: a large body of ice moving slowly down a slope or valley or spreading outward on a land surface.

gravity: a force that pulls objects to the earth.

graze: to eat grass.

H

habitat: the natural area where a plant or animal lives.

herbivore: an animal that eats only plants.

hibernate: to spend a period of time completely inactive in order to survive harsh conditions.

I

Ice Age: a period of time when glaciers covered a large part of the earth.

iceberg: a large piece of floating ice.

ice pack: a large area of ice formed during a period of many years and made of pieces driven together by wind, weather, moving glaciers, water, and other forces.

insect: an animal that has three body parts and six legs and its skeleton on the outside of its body. Many insects have wings. Grasshoppers, ants, ladybugs, and honeybees are all insects.

M

mammal: an animal such as a human, dog, or cat. Mammals are born live, feed milk to their young, and usually have hair or fur covering most of their skin.

migrate: to move from one habitat to another according to the season.

mineral: a naturally occurring solid found in rocks and in the ground. Rocks are made of minerals. Gold and diamonds are precious minerals.

O

orbit: the path that Earth takes around the sun.

P

Paleolithic: describes humans and their ancestors who used stone tools, until about 10,000 years ago. Also called the Stone Age.

permafrost: the tundra's permanently frozen layer of soil just beneath the surface of the ground.

Pleistocene: the time in the earth's history from about 2.5 million years ago to 10,000 years ago that experienced repeated ice ages.

pollen: a fine, yellow powder produced by flowering plants. Pollen is spread around by the wind, birds, and insects, and is needed by a flower to make a seed.

poncho: a cape that falls in the back and the front with a hole for the head.

pressure: the force made when something pushes against something else.

pyrite: a shiny yellow mineral used to start a fire.

R

reflector: a material that reflects light.

reflect: to bounce back.

reptile: an animal covered with scales that moves on its belly or on short legs. A snake, turtle, lizard, and alligator are all reptiles.

S

shelter: a place to live that protects a person from the weather.

sinew: a strong band of animal tissue that connects muscle to bone.

species: a group of living things that are closely related and produce young.

T

terrarium: a small enclosed habitat.

theory: an unproven idea that explains why something is the way it is.

tundra: the treeless Arctic land that is permanently frozen below the top layer of soil.

W

water cycle: the continuous movement of water from the earth to the clouds and back to the earth again.

water vapor: water as a gas, such as fog, steam, or mist.

ICE AGE SITES

The best way to learn about the Ice Age is to visit places that show the impact it had on our land and lives! Evidence of the Ice Age can be found in every part of the world. This list features sites in the United States. This list doesn't include every place to visit, but it's a great place to start!

ALABAMA
Russell Cave National Monument, Bridgeport
nps.gov/ruca/index.htm

ALASKA
Petroglyphs at Feniak Lake, Noatak National Preserve, Kotzebue
nationalparkstraveler.org/2011/09
/archaeologists-find-curious-prehistoric-artifacts-noatak-national-preserve8754

Musk Ox farm, Palmer
muskoxfarm.org

ARIZONA
Murray Springs Clovis Site, San Pedro National Riparian Conservation Area, Hereford
blm.gov/nlcs_web/sites/az/st/en/prog/NLCS/
SanPedroNCA.html

CALIFORNIA
La Brea Tar Pits, Los Angeles
tarpits.org/la-brea-tar-pits

COLORADO
Lamb Springs Archeological Preserve, Highlands Ranch
lambspring.org

CONNECTICUT
Mashantucket Pequot Museum and Research Center, Mashantucket
pequotmuseum.org/PermanentExhibits.aspx
or
Glacial Park
ct.gov/deep/cwp/view.
asp?a=2701&Q=451216&depNav_GID=1641

FLORIDA
Old Vero Beach Ice Age Site, Vero Beach
oviasc.org

GEORGIA
Ocmulgee National Monument, Macon
nps.gov/ocmu/index.htm

HAWAII
Lake Waiau on Maunakea, Hawaii
lovebigisland.com/quick-and-remarkable-facts-about-hawaii/lake-waiau

ILLINOIS
Principia College Science Center Mammoth Dig Display, Elsah
content.principia.edu/sites/mammoth/progress

INDIANA
Indiana Caverns, Corydon
indianacaverns.com

IOWA
Driftless Area National Wildlife Refuge, Elkader
fws.gov/endangered/
bulletin/2003/01-02/24-26.pdf

KANSAS
Ice Age Monument, Blue Rapids
travelks.com/listing/ice-age-monument/12837

KENTUCKY
Big Bone Lick, Union
parks.ky.gov/parks/historicsites/big-bone-lick

MAINE
Ice Age Trail–Orono
iceagetrail.umaine.edu/trail.htm

MINNESOTA
Ice Age trail
iceagetrail.org/ice-age-trail

MISSOURI
Mastodon State Historic Site, Imperial
mostateparks.com/park/mastodon-state-
historic-site

MONTANA
Glacier National Park, West Glacier
nps.gov/glac/index.htm

NEBRASKA
Hudson–Meng Fossil Bed, Chadron
fossilfreeway.net/hudson.php

NEW JERSEY
Jenny Jump State Forest, Hope
visitnj.org/trip-idea/remnants-ice-age-
northwest-new-jersey

NEW MEXICO
**White Sands National Monument,
Holloman AFB**
nps.gov/whsa/index.htm

OHIO
Glacier Ridge Park, Plain City
metroparks.net/parks-and-trails/
glacier-ridge

OREGON
Erratic Rock State Natural Site, Amity
oregonstateparks.org/index.cfm?do=parkPage.
dsp_parkPage&parkId=96

PENNSYLVANIA
Meadowcroft Rock Shelter, Avella
heinzhistorycenter.org/meadowcroft

RHODE ISLAND
Block Island
blockislandchamber.com/about

SOUTH CAROLINA
Edisto Beach State Park, Edisto Island
southcarolinaparks.com/edistobeach/
edistobeach-top5list.aspx

SOUTH DAKOTA
Mammoth Site of Hot Springs, Hot Springs
mammothsite.com

TENNESSEE
Gray Fossil Site and Museum, Gray
gfsm.handsonmuseum.org

TEXAS
Ladonia Fossil Park, Ladonia
cocladonia.org/ladonia-fossil-park.html

VIRGINIA
**Virginia Museum of Natural History,
Martinsville**
vmnh.net/ice-age

WASHINGTON
**Ice Age Floods National Geologic Trail,
Coulee Dam**
wsm.wsu.edu/discovery/index.php/tag/ice-age

WEST VIRGINIA
Organ Cave
organcave.com

WISCONSIN
1,200-mile Ice Age Trail
nps.gov/iatr/index.htm

WYOMING
Legend Rock Petroglyph Site, Thermopolis
astate.edu/a/museum/exhibits

QR CODE GLOSSARY

ESSENTIAL QUESTIONS

Introduction: Why is it cold in the winter and warm in the summer in many places?

Chapter 1: How much of the land where you live can't be used by plants and animals because it is covered by buildings or concrete?

Chapter 2: Why was it hard for people to believe the ice age theory at first?

Chapter 3: How have the animals around you adapted to survive?

Chapter 4: What would life be like if you had to make everything you use instead of buying it?

Chapter 5: Is there a best temperature for life on Earth?

METRIC CONVERSIONS

Use this chart to find the metric equivalents to the English measurements in this book. If you need to know a half measurement, divide by two. If you need to know twice the measurement, multiply by two. How do you find a quarter measurement? How do you find three times the measurement?

English	Metric
1 inch	2.5 centimeters
1 foot	30.5 centimeters
1 yard	0.9 meter
1 mile	1.6 kilometers
1 pound	0.5 kilogram
1 teaspoon	5 milliliters
1 tablespoon	15 milliliters
1 cup	237 milliliters

WITHDRAWN
Anne Arundel Co. Public Library